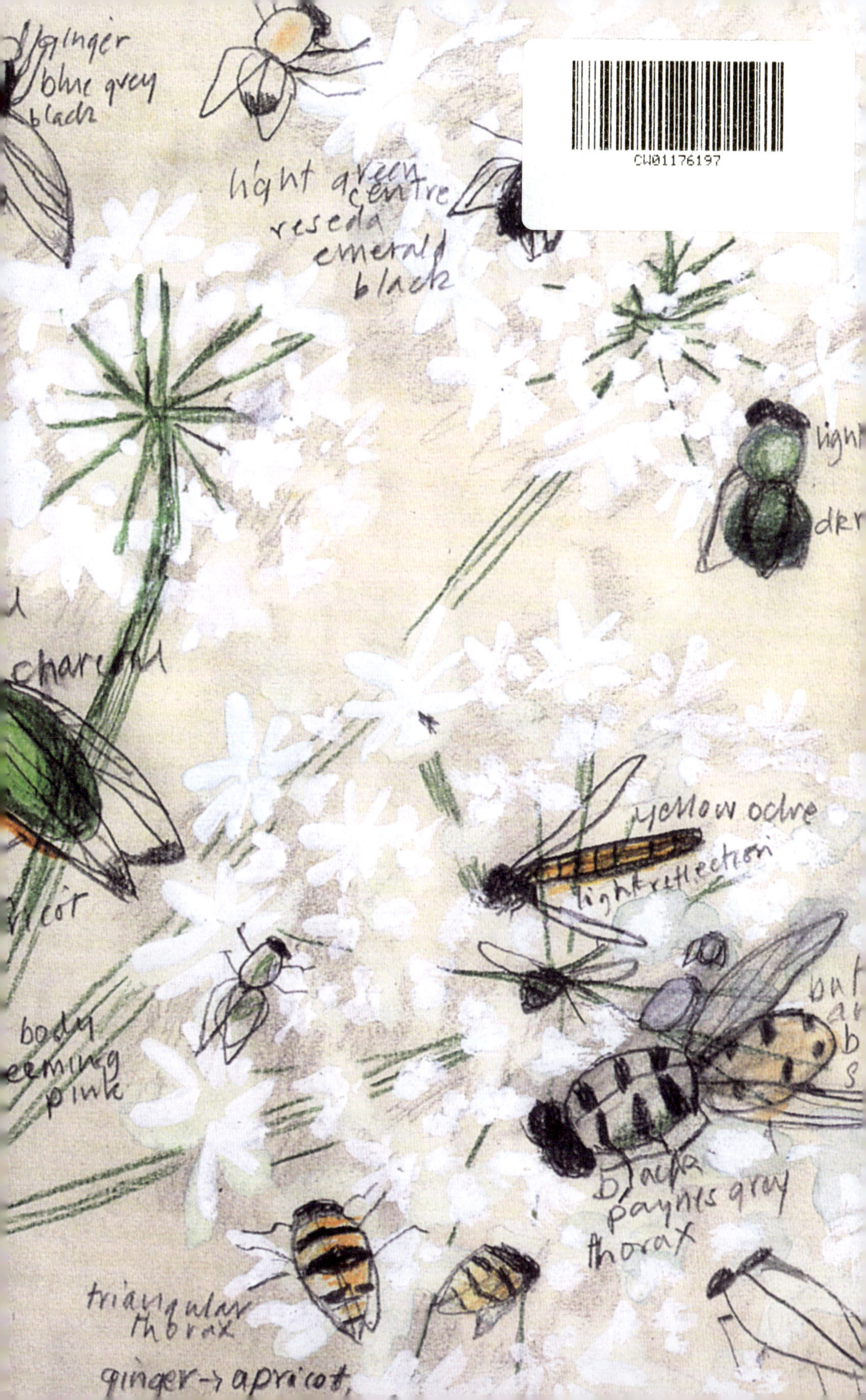
ginger
blue grey
black
light green centre
reseda
emerald
black
yellow ochre
light reflection
body
pink
black
paynes grey
thorax
triangular thorax
ginger → apricot,

AT HELPSTON

Ronald Blythe

First published in England 2011, Black Dog Books,
104 Trinity Street, Norwich, Norfolk, NR2 2BJ,
www.blackdogbooks.co.uk

Text © Ronald Blythe, Foreword © Edward Storey
Front Cover and other illustrations, © the estate of Mary Newcomb.

Frontispiece portrait of John Clare by W. Hilton, 1820, National Portrait Gallery
Photograph of the Behnes' bust of John Clare on p.153, © Peter Moyse
Photograph of John Clare on p.161, © Dorothy Rose

All rights reserved. No part of this publication may be reproduced, stored in a retrieval system, or transmitted in any form or by any means, electronic, mechanical, photocopying, recording or otherwise, without the prior permission of the copyright holders.

A CIP record of this book is available from the British Library.

ISBN 978-0-9565672-2-2

Printed in Great Britain by HSW Print, South Wales

AT HELPSTON

Meetings with John Clare

Ronald Blythe

Illustrations by Mary Newcomb

BLACK DOG
BOOKS

BY THE SAME AUTHOR

A Treasonable Growth
Immediate Possession and other stories
The Age of Illusion
William Hazlitt: Selected Writings
Akenfield
The View in Winter
Writing in a War
From the Headlands
The Stories of Ronald Blythe
Divine Landscapes
Private Words
Aldeburgh Anthology
Word From Wormingford
First Friends
Going to Meet George
Talking About John Clare
Out of the Valley
The Circling Year
Talking to the Neighbours
The Assassin
Borderland
A Writer's Day Book
Field Work
Outsiders
The Bookman's Tale
Aftermath: Selected Writings 1960-2010
At the Yeoman's House

MARY NEWCOMB

Mary Newcomb trained as a scientist. Her life as an artist was spent in the North-East Suffolk countryside. Her work was both wonderfully revealing and in a sense magical. No one had described rural England like this before. Her natural history landscape is unique and somehow private. I am grateful to her daughter Tessa, herself a remarkable artist, for permission to add these paintings to my John Clare book.

RB

Grassy Vetch

ACKNOWLEDGEMENTS

I am deeply in debt to all those who over these thirty years have made the John Clare Society what it is today, an exciting literary institution which attracts writers and artists, musicians and naturalists from all over the world – too many to name. Coming to Helpston has long been my favourite annual pilgrimage. These addresses are my own personal expressions of which I feel about John Clare. They are dependent on the scholarship of others. Part of my role has been to interpret this extraordinary rural voice as a fellow countryman, one whose boyhood saw the last vestiges of what he knew.

Ronald Blythe

I would like to thank the following for their help in the publication of *At Helpston*: Prof. John Goodridge, Nottingham Trent University; Robin Light, Crane Kalman Gallery and Peter Moyse, John Clare Society.

Peter Tolhurst, Black Dog Books

In Memoriam

Charles Causley
Michael Mayne

A flock of goldfinches dispersing 1993-5

CONTENTS

Foreword   11

Oceanic Clare   13
Clare in Hiding   19
Song   28
Kindred Spirits   35
John Constable and John Clare   42
Three Understandings   49
John Clare and the Paper Chase   55
Edmund Blunden and John Clare   65
The Ultimate Divide   71
John Clare and the Gypsies   79
Thomas Hardy and John Clare   88
John Clare in Scotland   101
The Helpston Boys   112
Solvitur ambulando: Clare and Footpath Walking   117
The Poet and the Nest   130
Clare's Two Hundredth Birthday   137
Signposts   141
Silent Likeness   148
Rider Haggard and the Disintegration of Clare's World   154

Bibliography   163
Index   165

This moth frightened me 1972

FOREWORD

Thirty-one years ago a small group of W.E.A. students, who had just attended a talk on the poetry of John Clare, decided to continue their discussion in the bar of the Fitzwilliam Arms, Castor. One of those members was the Reverend Brian Blade, the newly-appointed Rector of Helpston, who wanted to know why there wasn't a John Clare Society. 'After what I've heard this evening, I think there should be one.' In that relaxed atmosphere we all agreed it was a good idea and that letters should be sent to literary magazines and newspapers inviting anyone interested in Clare to get in touch with us.

I knew of several local people who would support us, including George Dixon and Rodney Lines, himself a W.E.A. lecturer and organiser. Both were enthusiastic and became founder-members. We then realised that such a society would need a head office, so Brian immediately offered the rectory as a venue for our first committee meetings. Having formed a committee it was then proposed that a prominent literary figure should be invited to become our President.

I had known the poet Charles Causley for several years and had taken him out to Helpston on two occasions when he came over from Cornwall to give poetry-readings in Peterborough. I remember sitting with him in the Bull Hotel on the evening he started his poem 'Helpston' – which he was to read later at the Service in Westminster Abbey when the Poet Laureate Ted Hughes unveiled the memorial plaque in Poets' Corner.

I thought Charles would be the ideal person to become our first President. He said he was honoured to be asked but did not want to be just a name on our letter-heading, adding 'Presidents should be involved and prepared to join in the battle.' But the journey from Launceston to Helpston was a long way to come for the many events he felt duty-bound to attend, so he had to say no.

At Helpston

Fortunately we had a mutual friend in Ronald Blythe who was equally enthusiastic about the Helpston poet and I wondered if he could be persuaded to be our first President. He replied in his usual quiet, modest way: 'Well, I'd love to, if you think I can be of any help.'

Thirty years later he is still in office and has done far more than just help. His annual Address at the Clare Festival each July immediately became one of the most important events of the day. His vast knowledge of rural traditions and country-writers meant he was able to reveal essential aspects of Clare's work that had previously received only a passing reference. We began to learn how, through the prose as well as the poetry, Clare could expand our awareness of the natural world. Our eyes were opened.

Today we are both fortunate and grateful that in this anniversary year, we have Ronnie's Presidential Addresses collected into one volume. They alone will prove what a wise and substantial contribution he has made to the Clare Society. Without his influence it is doubtful if Clare would have been given his place in Poets' Corner so soon, if at all.

What makes this publication even more worthy of our celebration is that all these thoughts on Clare have been given out of love for the poet, not only in Helpston but elsewhere. Those W.E.A. students chatting in the village pub all those years ago, would be amazed at what has happened since.

Edward Storey
Discoed
Powys
2011

OCEANIC CLARE

It is now thirty years since I, and a number of us here, formed the John Clare Society. Helpston has long been my favourite yearly outing. Its repetitive features have barely altered. Alan Cudmore and I set out early enough to collect Jane at Cambridge and to arrive at the John Clare Primary School by ten. The weather is invariably summery and the route exactly the same. As I sometimes imagine are the scant walkers we pass, for it is always Saturday. Jane is the widow of the Cambridge botanist Denis Garrett and whilst only mildly interested in our poet she adores Helpston itself because it where her grandmother Mrs Frank Perkins took her on picnics in the donkey cart. I had never seen Helpston – except from the Edinburgh train – before the Society was invented. But I knew all about it. The ruthless Enclosure Act had left it somewhat high, wide and handsome, and Clare's dolled-up birthplace denied all relationship with the dwelling in which he first glimpsed the light. When Edward Storey took Edmund Blunden to see it he had also to hurry him into the Blue Bell to recover from its previous transformation.

    I too had met Blunden in my twenties, and so of course had my old friend John Nash. He was retired to the Mill House at Long Melford which Siegfried Sassoon had given him. I am not certain that Blunden had given me his *Sketches in the Life of John Clare by Himself*, or if I began my interest in the great rural writer from this book, but the way to Helpston followed an autobiographical few miles towards his birthplace. Grandmother came from Long Melford, Cousin Winnie lived in Clare, and various life-long friends and acquaintances were dotted all the way to the Great North Road, aka the M1, tragically immortalised by Clare and unforgettably re-trodden by Iain Sinclair in his *Edge of the Orison* (2005). As Alan and I travelled it, and through the villages which ran to it, it was fetes and church flower festivals every few miles, but barely a walker. And of course that little ghost with wounded feet, and munching grass.

Coming home there would be supper in a pub or at Jane's, and later in Nayland, which was just three miles from Bottengoms Farm, and thus the pilgrimage ended, and thus the thirtieth begins. John Clare's travelling was constant. We would now be amazed by what distances were clocked-up by a nineteenth century farm labourer, both on the field and off. And in the poet's case just by skiving, a word he would not have encountered as it was invented in the 1915 trenches. But one of the benefits of Enclosure was that it left wild peripheries where one could read and write, or make love, or do nothing at all, without being seen. And which required long walks. Today's naturalists, such as Robert Macfarlane, now seek them out. Only a scrap of England is built over it is surprising to know. Not that one would credit this as one beats along the motorways to the Helpston lanes, as many of us have done since 1981.

Literary societies have a way of enlarging the understanding of a writer whilst stripping him down to the bone, and none more so than ours with John Clare. 'Poor Clare, poor Clare', I find myself saying as the latest analysis trickles in, my own included. Then what should we be doing to him on this our thirtieth birthday? I hazard that few writers this past hundred years have been so worked on, analysed, dissected, 'taught', promoted, ravaged for historic information or fictionalised as he. Natural history, agrarian facts, dialect, folksong, psychology, what you will, it is all there in Clare. We have his biography down to his last breath, which is amazing. It beguiles us because it is so much our biography too. We cannot have enough of it. Universities feed us with things about him as naturalist – Clare watched birds ceaselessly feeding their young. When will we grow up and take flight with him? Or do no more than read him? If only for a bit? When did any of us last look into Clare as John Keats looked into Chapman's Homer, hearing him 'speak out loud and clear', and having our entire universe expanded by his language?

George Chapman's translation of the *Odyssey* and the *Iliad* unbalanced Keats. Threw him. He was twenty-one, had passed one of his medical exams, had left the sulphurous Poultry for pure Hampstead and had decided to change his career, having come into a little money.

He needed to know something of the classics and his old schoolmaster at Enfield recommended this version of Homer. It was Enfield you will recall that the gypsies told Clare to turn to the Great North Road. Very soon both young men would turn to the same publishers and each would know of the other. I assumed I knew of both their poetry but until I read Chapman's Homer for the benefit of this thirtieth address I had no notion of why it should have knocked Keats sideways. He doesn't say that he had read it or studied it, merely that he had looked into it, and I see him warily opening, here and there his teacher's recommendation, put off may be by its size and classroom feel and then seeing this:

Calypso's Island

He stoopt *Pieres*, and thence
Glid through the aire; and *Neptune*'s Confluence
Kist as he flew, and chekt the waves as light
As any Sea-mew, in her fishing flight,
Her thicke wings soucing in the savorie seas.
Like her, he pass'd world of wildernesse;
But when the far-off Ile he toucht, he went
Up from the blue sea, to the Continent,
And reachd the ample Caverne of the Queene:
Whom he within found, without, seldome seene,
A Sun-like fire upon the harth did flame;
The matter precious, and divine the frame,
Of Cedar claft, and Incense was the Pile,
That breath'd an odour round about the Ile.
Her selfe was seated in an inner roome,
Whom sweetly sing he heard; and at her loome,
About a curious web, whose yarne she threw
In, with a golden shittle. A Grove grew
In endless Spring about her Caverne round,
With odorous Cypresse, Pines, and Poplars crownd.
Where Haulks, Sea-owles, and long-tongu'd Bittours bred,
And other birds their shadie pinions spread.
All Fowles maritimall; none roosted there,

At Helpston

> But those whose labours in the waters were.
> A Vine did all the hollow Cave embrace;
> Still greene, yet still ripe bunches gave it grace.
> Four fountains, one against another power'd
> Their silver streames; and meadowes all enflowed
> With sweet Balme-gentle, and blur Violets hid,
> That deckt the soft breasts of each fragrant Mead.
> Should any one (though he immortall were)
> Arrive and see the sacred objects there;
> He would admire them, and be over-joyd;
> And so stood *Hermes* Ravisht powres employd.
>   But having all admir'd, he enterd on
> The ample Cave; nor could be seene unknowne
> Of great *Calypso* (for all Deities are
> Prompt in each others knowledge; though so farre
> Severd in dwellings) but he could not see
> *Ulysses* there within. Without was he
> Set sad ashore; where 'twas his use to view
> Th' unquiet sea; sigh'd, wept, and emptie drew
> His heart of comfort.

George Chapman published his *The Whole Works of Homer, Prince of Poets* in 1616, the year Shakespeare died. Previous volumes had appeared before then and its magnificence, plus the opening up to Elizabethan shipping of oceanic prospects previously unimaginable, was entrancing Keats had studied classical literature via John Lemprière's *Classical Dictionary* (1788), his Apollo's 'realms of gold', yet,

> ...did I never breathe its pure serene
> Till I heard Chapman speak out loud and bold:
> Then felt I like some watcher of the skies
>   When a new planet swims into his ken;
> Or like stout Cortez when with eagle eyes
>   He stared at the Pacific – and all his men
> Look'd at each other with a wild surmise –
>   Silent, upon a peak in Darien.

Oceanic Clare

John Clare is a great sea of language which when it first came into view has been navigated by editors, traversed, wondered at but not always *read*. Much of his current appeal stems from his being us then, the nineteenth century villager, the ancestor who regularly shows up in the church registers as 'Labourer', the parson not being able to write for some strange reason ploughman, shepherd, stockman, forester, herdsman, etc. Clare, the spokesman for these skilled people of the fields, woods and pastures, would sometimes blame them for their 'condition' and dub them clowns. If he could look up and see the countryside, and themselves as part of its glories, then the world would become another place. They should study the wealth they held in common, birdsong, spring flowers, even Chapman's 'bittours' in the fenland cuts and sluices. Not far away another poet, George Crabbe, soon himself to be a country parson, thought it quite ordinary to find among the sailor-fieldworkers young men who were skilled botanists and naturalists generally. Who sang and made music, who were not 'low'. He himself believed that he 'had a right to song'.

But how do we, his twenty-first century descendants, find a peak in Darien from which to hear Clare's song as excitingly as John Keats heard George Chapman's Homer? Only by reading one's self into that notorious flood of words until a poem here and there holds us up, eventually steering us towards comprehension. And this can only be a self-taught journey. Finding Clare is not as simple as one thinks. Voluminous writers can be as furtive as his nightingale, singing best under cover. Authorities will map the way but it is best to follow one's own instincts. To read towards some place or places in that vast outpouring where poetry alone meets us and amazes us. Clare's universe often takes us 'out of our country' and into his, which can be bewildering. For the Clare traveller the map can be inexact. But then we might remember that it was not 'stout Cortez' who stood 'upon a peak in Darien' but a member of his expedition, Vasco Nunez de Balboa and who named the calm waters which spread before him the Pacific Ocean. Does this inexactitude diminish what John Keats saw when he looked into Chapman's Homer? Far from it. As when we privately, as it were, stare into the huge and far

At Helpston

from pacific country of John Clare, we are likely to find a peak which best suits us to comprehend it, for myself the bird poems and of course the apologias for his own existence, the flower poems and what I think of as the freedom poems in which he makes great if brief flights from the multiple restrictions of his time. My suggestion now is that for a time at least you and I should read more of him and less about him. One of the duties of poetry is to destroy our leaden certainties and startle us into a wild surmise.

As we know, not long after finding Ulysses listening to bittours on Calypso's isle, Keats would set sail for Italy. Neither he nor Clare believed that they had done enough to be remembered. 'Here lies one whose name was writ in water' –

> Into the nothingness of scorn and noise,
> Into the living sea of waking dreams
> Where there is neither sense of life or joys
> But the vast shipwreck of my life's esteems ...

The last bird home

CLARE IN HIDING

In his poem 'The Botanist's Walk', written at High Beach, Epping, Clare says of the nightingale 'She hides and sings', which I have often thought might well be a description of himself – 'He hides and sings'. Clare brought to a fine art the old village practice of vanishing in the local landscape. A village was, still is in some ways, the least private place on earth. A native village left one exposed and naked. To have kept an important side of oneself from the eyes and ears of the neighbours would have amounted to genius. To be 'different' as Clare was different was disastrous. In Suffolk we called it 'sticking out'. As we know, John Clare stuck out a mile, sometimes miserably, often not caring. Both tough and sensitive, both profoundly native and yet not belonging, he would occasionally rail about the locals, with their ceaseless gossip and prying, though never with surprise. They were the price he paid for living in paradise. He would play down the latter when away from Helpston and apologise for coming from such a dull place, and every now and then, when at home, he would lash out in ferocious criticism of its meanness, cruelty, injustice and grimness, such criticism being the anger he felt towards those who defiled their own nest, so to speak.

From boyhood on Clare led a double life at Helpston, a now-you-see-me, now-you-don't existence. During the course of giving a lecture on Francis Kilvert at Hereford, and mentioning Clare, someone spoke of the poet's East Midlands, seen from the train, as being 'a featureless plain for miles and miles'. But then his country was Kilvert country, the Wye Valley, the distant Black Mountains, a delectable border land, although as we know from Kilvert's Diary, a region with its own enchanting, and sometimes terrible, hideaways. A few weeks before this Alan Cudmore and myself had stopped for a picnic by the side of a lane just a couple of miles from Helpston, by

At Helpston

chance at a spot which neither of us had noticed before, to find ourselves all at once in a situation of classic John Clare secrecy. There was a group of oaks which would have been full grown in his day, a rutted grassy waste, an empty green lane – and a nightingale in full song. One could have watched the bird or read a book or written verses for hours on end without being seen by a soul. There are villages all over eastern England, like Helpston, which although seemingly laid out on a level which denies shelter or hiding place to those who needed to escape from the community, are full of spots where one can totally disappear.

There is a theme, an obsession, a burning necessity, which runs throughout Clare's poetry and prose, that of going into hiding. Not that he was alone in doing this. Such a disappearance trick was one of the great arts of the noisy, nosy, inquisitive old countryside. William Hazlitt, of whom Clare wrote a sharply observed profile, had practised such hiding away since he was a boy at Wem, when he would read all day long in the long grass, shutting his ears to cries from the manse. Not long ago I passed my neighbour idling at the far edge of his field and told him, 'Your wife is calling you.' 'I know she is,' he replied. John Clare had to get out of earshot and out of view in order to see and hear. At Dr Allen's no doubt rackety asylum with its inmates, attendants and servants, he wrote:

>   O take me from the busy crowd,
>   I cannot bear the noise;
>   For Nature's voice is never loud;
>   I seek for quiet joys.
>   (*Later Poems*, I, p.19)

It was at High Beach that he wrote a disturbing poem on how a patient from the asylum would affect the world outside.

>   I went in the fields with the leisure I got
>   The stranger might smile but I heeded him not
>   The hovel was ready to screen from a shower
>   And the book in my pocket was read in an hour

> The bird came for shelter but soon flew away
> The horse came to look and seemed happy to stay
> He stood up in quiet and hung down his head
> And seemed to be hearing the poem I read
>
> The ploughman would turn from his plough in the day
> And wonder what being had come in his way
> To lie on a molehill and read the day long
> And laugh out aloud when he finished his song
>
> Fame bade me go on and I toiled the day long
> Till the fields where he lived should be known in my song
>   (*Later Poems*, I, p.26)

One day Clare lists his own ecstasies, imaginations and hopes. Here is an inventory of delights—delights which he shared only with some of his fellow Helpstonians but which he believed should be shared by all. Orchis hunting. Gypsies. Old stone pits fringed with ivy. Gathering cowslips for wine. The pleasure of waiting in a spot to hear the song of the nightingale. Waiting for a lover. The successive growth of flowers – he means the discovering of a certain flower, such as the white violet, in the same place year after year. The pleasures of fair-going in boys. The pleasures of cutting open a new book on a spring morning. The pleasures of lovers walking narrow lanes. House-warming customs. Birds-nest building. Larks. The pleasure of the shepherd making marks to tell by the sun the time of the day. The pleasure of the boy angling over the bridge, and of boys stripping off to jump over a cat gallows. The pleasures of schoolboys climbing the leads of the church to cut their names there. The pleasures of pelting at the weather cock. The pleasure of an old man taking a journey to see his favourite oak gathering into leaf.

    Clare's study of natural history began in solitude but it eventually opened out into consultation, the more so when Taylor his publisher suggested that he wrote a 'Selborne' for Helpston. Where the village was concerned, his learned interest in plants and birds made him less strange than his regularly vanishing into the wilds to read and scribble. It had no idea how sacred Helpston itself was to him, and that his

At Helpston

vanishings were like the withdrawal from the crowd of a contemplative who needed to feed on silence. Just before the fatal move to Northborough so like was he to his 'successive growth flowers' that he might well have been off to Botany Bay – he wrote defensively, 'There are some things that I shall regret leaving, and some journeys that I shall make yearly – to see the flood at Lolham Briggs, to gather primroses in Hilly Wood, and hunt the nightingale's nest in Royce Wood, and to go to see the furze in flower on Emmonsails Heath.'

In lieu of what was soon to befall him at Northborough, we can see in this constant listing of his birthplace's secret glories in what he called his 'solitudes', and the intellectual and sensuous responses which they accorded, his own statement of what he knew he possessed, even in the madhouse, his true identity card. There it was, the interior document which showed half his life in the blessed woods and fields, half his life in hell.

> O could I be as I have been
>   And ne'er can be no more
> A harmless thing in meadows green
>   Or on the wild sea shore
>
> O could I be what once I was
>   In heaths and valleys green
> A dweller in the summer grass
>   Green fields and places green
>
> A tenant of the happy fields
>   By grounds of wheat and beans
> By gipsies camps and milking bield
>   Where luscious woodbine leans ...
>
> I wish I was what I have been
>   And what I was could be
> As when I roved in shadows green
>   And loved my willow tree

> To gaze upon the starry sky
>   And higher fancies build
> And make in solitary joy
>   Loves temple in the field
>   (*Later Poems*, I, p.193)

At Helpston Clare sought different solitudes, one for nature study, one for 'escape', one for inspiration, one for reading, one for bliss. The uncultivated region beyond the enclosure, the Hills and Holes at Barnack, the muddles and sunken ponds, all became a set of outdoor studies where he could safely close the door on noise and intrusion. He is the human nightingale who hides and sings.

> While I wander to contrive
> For myself a place as good
> In the middle of a wood
> There aside some mossy bank
> Where the grass in bunches rank
> Lifts its down on spindles high
> Shall be where I choose to lie
>   ('Noon', *Selected Poems and Prose*, p.5)

But other things belonging to what might have been often intrude into these hides, such as Mary Joyce's voice, whose 'beautiful tone ... made loneliness more than alone'. It was often the fate of the religious who went to hear God in desert silences to hear instead some other, unbearable, voice.

John Clare frequently rationalises his need to hide with that of the wild creatures. 'Nightingales are very jealous of intrusions and their songs are hymns to privacy'. He often sees himself like 'the time-killing shepherd boys whose summer homes are ever out of doors' and he celebrates their workaday (and workanight) freedom in two splendid poems, 'A Sunday with Shepherds and Herdboys' and 'Shepherds Hut'. He likes the idea that 'The pewits are hid from all sight but the allseeing sun' and that the martin cat 'hides in lonely shade / where prints of human foot is scarcely made', that the

At Helpston

hedgehog hides beneath the rotting hedge, and that 'each nimbling hare / Sturts quick as fear and seeks its hidden lair'. Though the robin seems to be fond of company and the haunts of men, and makes no secret of its dwelling. Yet when he writes 'The Robin's Nest' he makes it a poem to solitude. Helpston, clogging away on the land, finds him timewasting and problematical. Often in village terms he is a skiver. Even when sharing its normal toil:

> I homeward used to hie
> With thoughts of books I often read by stealth
> Beneath the blackthorn clumps at dinner hour
>   ('Labours Leisure', *Selected Poetry and Prose*, p.104)

The village would have understood that other stealth which he wrote about. Until quite recently the woods and meadows were erotic. Noting a daisy in some flattened grass, Clare wrote:

> Might well e'en Eve to stoop adown and show
> Her partner Adam in the silky grass
> This little gem that smiled where pleasure was
>   ('The Eternity of Nature', *Selected Poetry and Prose*, p.110)

Arm-in-arm courting along the footpaths and lanes was the public statement of the clandestine lovemaking which took place in the secret tangles and wastes. One day Clare would write, wryly, 'The pleasures of youth are enjoyed in youth only'.

  Soon he would be obliquely describing himself as 'the man of science', and with some justification. For his publisher James Hessey too was recommending him to read Gilbert White. Not that Hessey ever had any great faith in what Clare might do in this direction, but it was a percipient notion all the same. Yet there were dangers. 'I would have you be careful how you venture in Prose ... you may injure your Poetical Name by a prose attempt'. But as Margaret Grainger points out in her *The Natural History Prose Writings of John Clare*, publishers like John Taylor and James Hessey could have had little or no comprehension of the intellectual field into which Clare had been taken by Edmund Artis and Joseph Henderson. All three of them had become indeed 'men of science'. Helpston itself positively welcomed the news that Clare was collecting information on birds and beasts and flowers, and was eager to contribute. 'The winter before last one of Phillips draymen of the common brewhouse Stamford, when coming to Helpston, saw a strange bird in Pilsgate meadow ... a schoolmaster was at a public-house & tho he had Pennants History he declared that he was unable to call it by its name.' It could have been a young heron or a gannet. As for Clare's prose, it is frequently electric. He is the master of the startled moment, of the confrontation between himself and the surprised creature which he is stalking. He is not at all like Gilbert White. Although he now is 'the man of science' he remains the birds-nesting boy and the bird-like hiding poet. It often embarrassed him to be caught-out doing youthful things when he was a grown-up. 'I feel almost ashamed of my childish propensities and cannot help blushing if I am observed by a passing neighbour'.

With a possible John Clare's *Natural History of Helpstone* on the stocks, and with the locals finding it an acceptable task, his excursions need no longer be fugitive. When the village saw him, day after day, and even late at night, making for his hides, it made sense to them. They chose to forget that their man of science had previously been notorious for loving 'each desolate neglected spot / That seems in labours left forgot', and had sought relief in finding places which neither plough nor woodman, railway navvy nor roadmaker had violated. It thrilled him to the heart to discover some unreclaimed spot. He moved stealthily among these wastes which had become nature's own enclosures in acts of consecration 'The sacredness of mind in such deep solitudes we seek – and find'. He joins what he calls their 'heirs and tenants'. He wrote,

> I felt it happiness to be
> Unknown, obscure and like a tree
> In woodland peace and privacy
> ('The Progress of Rhyme', *Selected Poetry and Prose*, p.124)

At Helpston

And he is intrigued by seeing the behaviour of someone, such as the cow boy, who gives vent to his feelings when he thinks himself unobserved.

> Absorbed as in some vagrant summer dream
>   And now in gestures wild
> Starts dancing to his shadow on the wall
>   Feeling self gratified
>   Nor fearing human thrall
> ('Summer Images', *Selected Poetry and Prose*, p.148)

It was of course this habit of lying low from childhood which made John Clare a naturalist. He was from the very beginning on the level of 'different insects passing and repassing as if going to market or fair, some climbing up bents and rushes like so many church steeples, and others getting out of the sun and into the bosom of a flower'.

Soon he would be hidden away until the end of his life, though not in solitude. That must have been the worst horror of it. He wrote himself out of this worst of all isolation, and incessantly, to bring back the old hiding places, a girl's voice and the wild birds' songs, and an uncontaminated air. He had always loved the Book of Job and now he tasted its despair. In 'The Nightingale's Nest', among his finest achievements, he says;

> – How subtle is the bird! she started out
> And raised a plaintive note of danger nigh
> Ere we were past the brambles and now, near
> Her nest, she sudden stops – as choaking fear
> That might betray her home So even now
> We'll leave it as we found it – safety's guard
> Of pathless solitudes shall keep it still.
> See there she's sitting on an old oak bough
> Mute in her fears, our presence doth retard
> Her joys and doubts turns all her rapture chill
> Sing on, sweet bird, may no worse hap befall
> Thy visions than the fear that now deceives

House martins at our house in Linstead

SONG

It is late September, wild and dull, and I am in a great garden which stretches across England and Wales on both banks of the River Lugg to plant a tree for Trevor Hold. His passing surprised us, to my mind he looking so robust. His music was played as I heeled-in a commemorative tree. It was where Herefordshire joins Powys. From high Stockenny Farm you can see the Malvern Hills. The poet Edward Storey had lured him to this place. They were Clare country men who, like myself, were part of an annual festival at Discoed. Trevor Hold had dedicated a sonata to me. It had long been an amazing gift. And now that large amiable presence had vanished. The Helpston festival had barely started when he wrote this about John Clare and Music, he being the only one with the authority to do so. He called it 'The Composer's Debt to John Clare'.

'Amongst his other talents, John Clare was one of our most musical poets. English poets on the whole do not have much of a reputation for musical literacy. Those who could read music and play a musical instrument can be counted on the fingers of two hands. Though he had no academic musical training, Clare could play the fiddle – one of his most valued possessions was a Cremona violin given to him by his publisher James Hessey – and could 'prick down' (notate) tunes. Of more importance from the composer's point of view, he knew how to write words for musical setting. He acquired skill in this difficult art, like his beloved Burns before him, by writing new verses to existing tunes – to the old songs and 'halfpenny ballads' that his father had sung to him as a boy. As a writer of words-for-music, a 'lyric poet' in the original sense of the term, he has few rivals in nineteenth century England. His song-lyrics are extremely varied, ranging from love-songs to drinking-songs, from songs of remembered joys to songs of desolation and despair, from songs about birds, animals and flowers, to songs about songs. He brought to these lyrics and eye for detail rarely found: 'eyebright words, sharp as a camera'. Not for him the fey, pastoral worlds of Phyllis and Corydon. His farm-labourers have mud on their boots. His maidens sit not in Arcadian bowers but on molehills. He finds as much beauty in a bean flower as in a wild rose.'

Little wonder, then, that Clare has proved such an attraction to the composer. Indeed, *Poems Descriptive of Rural Life and Scenery* was still fresh from the press when Haydn Corri (1785-1860) produced his setting of *The Meeting*. Despite the parental hopes entrusted in his forename, Corri was a feeble composer and his song has a hot-house feeling about it quite at odds with the simplicity of the lyric. Clare could himself have been lucky to have missed Madame Vestris' performance of *Here we meet too soon to part* at Covent Garden on the night he arrived for his first visit to the capital. 'We was to have but it was too late.'

And I was to have had many more Border talks about music with Trevor Hold but it was too late. So here I was, shovelling the English-Welsh soil around his tree. Later we drove to Stockenny Farm to see Elgar's hills, lavender-coloured in the distance, and that marvellously sequential landscape of George Herbert, Henry Vaughan and Thomas Traherne. And of Clyro and Francis Kilvert from which I explored the Black Mountain, and that terrible sloping meadow where the Welsh women mutilated the fallen English, a deed so appalling that Shakespeare in the opening of *King Henry the Fourth, Part One*, shrank from describing it. Wild Glendower had conquered Mortimer.

> A thousand of his people butchered;
> Upon whose dead corpse there was such misuse,
> Such beastly shameless transformation,
> By those Welshwomen done, as may not be
> Without much shame re-told or spoken of.

Edward Storey and I climbed this innocent hill, he breaking off some Clare conversation to tell me that it was a battleground. Nearby was Offa's Dyke, white with sheep. Also Presteigne with its musicians.

On the whole the numerous composers who set Clare's poems did

At Helpston

not set those he called 'Song'. Sterndale Bennett set 'Winter's Gone'. Peter Warlock, Edmund Rubbra, Martin Shaw, Ian Copley, Stephen Dodgson and Gordon Jacob all set 'Little Trotty Wagtail', a poem written on 9th August 1849, presumably in Northampton Asylum. 'And tittering tottering sideways he near got straight again'. The Westminster Abbey choir would have sung Benjamin Britten's setting of 'The Evening Primrose' at the Poets' Corner service but having paid for the stone we could not afford it. Eric Robinson observed how critical opinion has changed since Clare attracted composers, and that there are more critics today 'who will make a strong case for Clare's many Songs than there were half a century ago'. Clare's Song-girls are partly traditional ballad-girls and partly vehicles for his sexual feelings. He had made love to women since he was fourteen, was married with seven children, and those feelings stayed with him, and could be expressed in 'Song'. Towards the end of that lengthy incarceration he wrote,

>   I live and love as others do
>   But seldom have the face to woo

Unlike all those fantasy females of Song this one sings! Who was she? Although possessing

>   Those swelling breasts like billows rise
>   To fascinate my wondering eyes

She steps out of the convention.

>   The voice I hear in music tones
>   Is thrilling through my very bones
>   The harp and lute & songs of choice
>   Are discord to her sweet young voice
>   So softly natural and so kind
>   Sweet woman she's a child in mind

A fellow patient? And in the same poem his ever-present dilemma?

Song

> A silent pain my heart doth fill
> It pants within but does not kill
> Love's a tormenting thing to seek
> Withering a heart it cannot break.

Clare would brush aside any deep meaning to his Song. 'When a face pleased me, I scribbled a song or so in her praise.' And Eric Robinson said that those poems were addressed not only to individuals but to Woman. 'How often did Clare have music in his head as he composed his Songs as he did when he composed one of the first "The Jewel of All"? And that even without their music, many of these Songs have a perfect lyrical quality.' Which is true. As you read, you sing. He lived at a time when everyone sang, there being no one to sing for them other than in the theatre. How often in church at weddings and funerals I see rows of the under-fifties not singing, they having only listened to singing, and this incessantly. A youthful conductor goes into the lion's den of a big non-singing comprehensive school to make it sing. The pupils are acutely embarrassed and have to be seduced into Song.

Clare would have heard his fellow inmates, both at Dr Allen's Asylum and at Northampton, singing, sometimes crazily, more likely beautifully and naturally, as they lived out their strange days. No drugs to keep them quiet, no difficulty in raising a song. At Helpston young people especially sang. All through Clare's *Shepherd's Calendar* they are singing. There his Song is to free girls. But then would come dream girls, girls borrowed from Robert Burns, wild women from gypsy encampments, but most of all wonderful imaginary women which could be his alone, who lived within music and who could be angelic or in his arms.

> Her bubbies they were lovely to see
> More than the sight of heaven could be
> Eve's was not more white than they
> The most angelic form of clay.

And of course he mentions 'The foggy, foggy dew' and we hear the burst of laughter in the Blue Bell. He wonders what it would be like to

At Helpston

be a girl so his Song is the erotic one of the Sailor's Return.

But is through Scottish balladry that John Clare claims his ancestry. There is a rich and accurate skirling tunefulness in this Song which spells freedom. It frees him from Northampton, taking him out of himself and into his heritage. He writes fluent Scottish dialect and a mock-Burns which could be Burns. It is a language which takes him home. How amazing it could have been if he had not walked from Epping to Northants but the other direction, from there to the Border. Once across, no one could ever capture him. His northern Song is itself liberating. If only he could have seen Scotland! This is what one feels as one reads it.

> Can ye love Lowland Lassie the lad i' the plaiden,
>   Can ye love the low shielden by the side o' the hill?
> Can ye love me, a Scotchman, my ain bonny maiden?
>   There the rock on its shieling is hanging there still.

And then John Clare would return to the Fens with all his native acceptance of them. He is their greatest voice. They need him otherwise the world would be unable to see them. He remembers how

> The rawh of the Autumn hangs over the woodland
> Like smoke from a City sulphurously grey,
> The heronshaw lonely hangs over the floodland
> And cranks its lone story throughout the dull day.
> Theres no green on the hedges, no leaves on the darkwood,
> No cows on the pasture or sheep on the lea.
> The Linnets cheep still, and how happy the Lark would
> Sing songs to sweet Susan to remind her of me.

If we do not 'hear' the Song from the asylum, listen to it's musicality, but just read it as a repetitive kind of nineteenth century 'pop', then we lose everything. Clare is singing in his writing, composing in his words. His emotional life is either all behind him and only to be remembered, or all before him in Scotland. We should hear these poems because he heard them, as singing voices – siren voices when they came from the North, familiar voices when they came from only just down the road. Women so near and yet so far to be sung to, to be longed for one way or the other. There is no escape.

> O had we never loved one another,
> We had neer been cursed together,
> Never shunned and never hated,
> Had we never been created.
>
> Woman in her own true nature
> Is a fair and lovely creature,
> Man a savage from the wild,
> But when loved a very child.

And when we read lines such as

> We stood beneath the hazel shade,
> Her arms lapp'd in her apron white

Clare's melancholy seems to anticipate that of Thomas Hardy in his 1912 Farewell poems to his wife Emma.

Song – a poem. A sound as of singing. *Oxford English Dictionary*

'He was likewise fond of Ballads, and I have heard him make a boast of it over his horn of ale, with his merry companions, that he could sing or recite above a hundred; he had a tolerable good voice, and was often called upon to sing at those bacchanalian merry makings.'

Clare on his father Parker Clare.

'For till my arrival at Casterton [where he met his wife Patty] my dealing with love was but temporary. When a face pleased me, I scribbled a song or two in her praise, try'd to get in her company, for the sake of pastime merely, as it's called, on a Sunday eve a time or two, and then left off, for new allurements in fresh faces, that took my fancy as superiors. These trifles were as innocent and harmless as trifling had I kept free from all others. Temptations were things that I rarely resisted, when the partiality

At Helpston

of the moment gave no time for reflection, I was sure to seize it, whatever might be the consequences ... Perhaps it's not improper or too insignificant to mention that my first feelings of love was created at school, even while a boy. A young girl, I may say a child, won my affections not only by her face, which I still think very handsome, but by her meek, modest and quiet dispositions, – the stillest and most good-natured girl in the school. Her name was Mary, and my regard for her lasted a long time after school days were over, but it was a platonic affection, nothing else but love in idea, for she knew nothing of my fondness for her, no more than I did of her inclinations to forbid or encourage me had I disclosed afterwards. But other Marys &c., excited my admiration, and the first creator of my warm passions was lost in a perplexed multitude of names, that would fill a volume to calendar them all down, ere a bearded chin could make the lawful apology for my entering the lists of Cupid. Thus began and ended my amorous career ... My faults I believe to be the faults of most people ... Virtue or innocence, pretending perfection in this world, is to common sense a painted sepulchre.

Sketches in the Life of John Clare written by Himself
Edited by Edmund Blunden, 1931

The 'stillest' girl was Mary Joyce his muse, and who he came to regard as his real wife.

A delicate balance

KINDRED SPIRITS

History has its wilful side. It refuses to stay within its dates. Parts of it trickle on into decades – even centuries – where, to the historian, it doesn't belong. Somebody says something and a connection is made by which history, whether social, or literary, or political, stops being History with a capital H and a discipline, and becomes something which is still happening. Then writers, novelists, poets, dramatists confuse us by not playing the history game according to the historians' rules. Thomas Hardy's novels rushed out one after another in roughly twenty years between the 1870s and 1890s yet without being 'historical' were a reflection of early nineteenth-century Dorset – his mother's countryside. My Suffolk grandparents were born in 1860, when Clare was still living, and before Hardy had written a word. My grandmother lived to watch our first television set, when she was nearly a hundred years old. 'I have to ask one thing', she said, 'can *they* see *us*?' A good question.

I had never heard of Clare as a boy. 'Our' poet was Robert Bloomfield. I used to bike to Honington to look at the cottage in which he was born. It was very like the house in which I was born, which was thatched and beamed, with a big garden, a horse-pond, pig-sties, outside lavatory – two holes so that mother could sit with a child – fruit trees and a well. It doesn't exist now. Three executive bungalows stand on the site. One can trace the horse-pond where the stripy lawn dips. By the side of the house is the long beech avenue from the lane to the vicarage up which my parents were driven in the borrowed vicarage carriage in 1920 after their wedding. They were twenty-three, and my father had been at Gallipoli and was now returning to a broken-down agriculture. Not far away were two young writers I would one day meet, Edmund Blunden and Adrian Bell.

But it was the long-dead but still strangely influential writer Robert Bloomfield who was one of the haunters of my childhood. He was

At Helpston

born in 1766 and so belonged to a previous generation to Clare. His father was a village tailor and his mother a village schoolteacher. For all that, he was barely literate when he joined his two elder brothers in London to be apprenticed as a shoemaker. The three brothers and four other men all lived and worked in one room in great squalor. Bloomfield was short and slight, but not with Clare's 'smallness', being shaped by malnutrition and toil. Being blunted in fact. Bloomfield taught himself English by reading the speeches of Burke, Fox and North in the London newspapers. Eventually a Scot named Kay joined the crowded shoemakers and brought with him a copy of *Paradise Lost* and – need I tell you – Thomson's *The Seasons*. So the little Suffolk poet was away. He sent some verses called 'The Milkmaid' to the *London Magazine* and they were accepted. He then began to compose *The Farmer's Boy*, managing to hold as many as 50 to 100 lines in his head before he could move from his last and write them down. Bloomfield wrote the whole of this long poem whilst working alongside the hammering, sewing, chattering men. Old people still knew fragments of it by heart when I was a child. It went to bookseller after bookseller (i.e. publisher) for years and eventually ended up with a Mr Capel Lofft from the poet's own part of Suffolk. In 1798 Capel Lofft wrote a preface to *The Farmer's Boy*, had it illustrated and got it published. It sold 26,000 copies. This bestseller – alas – haunted those who were later to publish John Clare as a second Bloomfield, notwithstanding Clare's greatness.

Clare himself honoured Bloomfield as writers from shared circumstances frequently honour each other. He would also have known about the tragedy which overtook Bloomfield. There is a saying in East Anglia, 'He rose too high – so he fell'. Bloomfield's career bleakly acknowledges this logic. After the fame of *The Farmer's Boy* the Duke of Grafton got him a position as an under-sealer at the Seals Office but the poet wasn't able to keep it. The Duke then gave him a shilling a day. Bloomfield was married now, the children coming along. He wrote further books, all of which failed and the slide into penury was fast. He then became bankrupt. There was a fashion for Aeolian harps, brought about by the Grecian revival, and Bloomfield tried to make a living by creating these. One of his harps is in Moyses's

Hall, Bury St. Edmunds. Also his writing table. The Aeolian harp was set up in gardens so that the wind could pass through the strings and produce musical sounds. The sound was like that of the wind in telephone wires. Nobody bought Bloomfield's harps, and nobody seemed to notice the irony of a poet having to give up language and try to support himself – by wind. His harps were beautifully crafted.

Bloomfield's biographer in the *Dictionary of National Biography* says that he 'lacked independence and manliness, and would have gone mad had he lived any longer', a cruel verdict and an unfair one. He died in great poverty and distress in 1823, a short while after John Clare had reached the pinnacle of his brief popularity with *Poems Descriptive of Rural Life and Scenery* written by 'a Northamptonshire Peasant'. At the last Bloomfield was so wretchedly ill and poor that he tried to touch the heart of his readers by begging them to buy his book *Wild Flowers* because the royalties would provide a financial crutch for his crippled only son. In this world of sick and starving – and socially humiliated – writers we are in a 'history' that no amount of late twentieth-century scholarship can quite succeed in bringing home to us. John Clare, of course, would have exactly understood. He called Robert Bloomfield a 'sweet unassuming minstrel' and wrote:

> The tide of fashion is a stream too strong
> For pastoral brooks that gently flow and sing
> But nature is their source and earth and sky
> Their annual offering to her current bring
> *(Middle Poems*, IV, p.182-3)

The trouble for certain poets and artists at the turn of the nineteenth century was that the English rural scene was commonplace. The new middle classes which sprang up after the Napoleonic Wars did not want Constable's pictures of farms in their new houses. Haywains cooled their axles in every ford and pond. When Constable died in 1837 he left a house full of unsold work. His two uncles – his father's brothers – lived in my present village and ground the corn from the fields which once belonged to my farmhouse, and are buried in the churchyard. He called them 'the Wormingford folk'. Their handsome

At Helpston

tombs, half hidden in honeysuckle, proclaim their status – 'Gent'. I was struck when reading Mrs Constable's letters to her son John, then attempting to establish himself as a painter in London, by the near-absence of reference to the village people of East Bergholt, who only get a mention if they have an accident or might be prosecuted. Constable's placid (his favourite word) territory was threatened by rural unrest. He strove to show the grandeur and the reality of scenery, but was detached from the men and women whose toil produced the sumptuousness and order which he loved. His farmhouses take precedence over the labourers. The superb painting called 'The Leaping Horse', originally 'The Jumping Horse', however, was a horror picture for a society which, above anything else, was terrified of what to them looked like an uncontrolled horse. But the great artist was here showing his accurate eye for a workaday and yet very beautiful world. Every half-mile or so along the towpaths of the River Stour there was a wicket fence to the water's edge to stop sheep and cattle straying. When the huge Suffolk Punches which drew the Constables' barges encountered such a fence, the bargee would give a low whistle and the largest horses in England – leapt!

John Clare, unlike Robert Bloomfield, made few concessions to 'taste' when it came to describing the actualities of village life, and was famously the despair of patrons and publishers alike. But Bloomfield is unusually impressive in his dealing with illness. He is the poet of rural sickness without ever quite realising it. He catches in his verse the tell-tale cough, the crippled walk, the flight of strength. One of his most interesting poems in this respect is *Good Tidings; or News from the Farm*. What are these good tidings? They are that Dr. Jenner has discovered a vaccine in 'the harmless cow'. 'We shall look back upon smallpox as the scourge of days gone by'.

Bloomfield's death in 1823 upset Clare. There had been certain curious cross-references before Clare's publishers sought to present him as a genius from the same mould. For example, at the brief height of Bloomfield's fame an illustrated edition of his poetry was issued containing views not only of Norfolk and Suffolk, but of *Northamptonshire*. This was *Views...Illustrative of the Works of Robert Bloomfield*, and the artists were John Greig and James Storer. This in

Kindred Spirits

1806, when Clare was only thirteen.

It would have been fascinating to know if Clare ever saw a Constable during his 1820s visits to London. John Clare's artist was Edward Rippingille, a wild blade five years his junior. During the London visits the pair of them went on the town, drinking and looking for girls. Rippingille had a reckless reputation in his adopted city Bristol. Clare was very fond of him:

> He is a rattling sort of odd fellow with a desire to be thought one and often affects to be so for the sake of singularity and likes to treat his nearest friends with neglect and carlessness on purpose as it were to have an oppertunity of complaining about it
>
>   he is a man of great genius as a painter and what is better he has not been puffed into notice like the thousands of farthing rush lights (like my self perhaps) in all professions that have glimmered their day and are dead I spent many pleasant hours with him in London   his greatest rellish is pun[n]ing over a bottle of ale for he is a strong dealer in puns ... we once spent a whole night at Offleys the Burton ale house and sat till morning (*By Himself*, pp.137-8)

The critics were ruthless. Rippingille, they said, 'allowed his garden, the musing of an owl, his guitar, his building and firing at a mark with a pistols, to encroach too much on his afternoons – which he calls days'.

John Clare was all for a young man who called his afternoons days, and who played a guitar while listening to owls. Shades of Edward Lear. Clare also maintained 'that no artist had such a true English conception of real pastoral life and *reality* of English manners as Rippingille'. He was the son of a King's Lynn farmer and Clare remembered once seeing a shop full of his paintings in Wisbech in 1809.

Rippingille knew the Eltons of Clevedon Court, near Bristol and I am indebted to the late Lady Elton for the concluding part of this lecture. For it is about her husband's ancestor, Sir Charles Abraham Elton's percipient understanding of John Clare, and about a strange poem he wrote to him after seeing him on one of his unhealthy London forays– during the zenith days. Lady Elton wrote to me on 13th August 1993:

At Helpston

The Clare-Elton friendship is rather complicated. They seem to have met in London c.1822 at the monthly Dinner for contributors to the *London Magazine*, and with Rippingille the Bristol painter, went to Astley's Circus where they saw 'morts of tumbling', to Deaville the phrenologist to have their heads cast in plaster, and to boxing matches. This is all described (I think) in a letter not in Tibble, but in the British Library. When Clare was back in Helpston c.1824 Charles Elton sent him a copy of his *Epistle To John Clare*, urged him to come to Bristol, and promised that Rippingille would paint his portrait. Family tradition has it that Charles Elton sent Clare five guineas, although he was relatively poor.

He had married in 1804 against his father's wishes, the Rev. Sir Abraham being a Hellfire and Brimstone Evangelical who refused to help him. By 1825 he had eleven extant children, including two sets of identical twins. The two eldest boys were drowned in Weston in 1819, hence the poem 'Boyhood: A Monody' published in 1820. It so impressed John Scott that Charles Elton was invited to become a contributor to the *London Magazine*, taken over by Taylor and Hessey when Scott was killed in a duel. The money was very useful as Charles Elton was living on half-pay as an officer in the Somerset Militia. Henry Hallam, his brother-in-law, also helped to support one family. (Henry's son Arthur's early death inspired Tennyson's *In Memoriam*. Tennyson was at work on his poem whilst living near John Clare at Epping. The New Year bells of 'Ring out, wild bells' are those of Waltham Abbey.)

By 1825 Charles Elton felt that he could afford Thomas Barker's fee of £100 to have his wife and children painted in Bath, a fetching series of portraits which we still have. The next year Rippingille painted 'The Travellers' Breakfast', ostensibly in a Bristol Inn, and a jokey picture, as Wordsworth, Dorothy Wordsworth and Coleridge are in it, though they had long since left Bristol. Lamb, Southey, Cottle, Charles Elton, four of his daughters, his wife and two infant sons, Rippingille himself, *and*, I am convinced, a lithe rustic figure as Clare...

This is how Charles Elton's poem-invitation to visit him in Somerset opens. It was first published in the *London Magazine* in

Kindred Spirits

August 1824, and subsequently in *Boyhood and Other Poems and Translations* in 1835.

Epistle to John Clare

So loth, friend John! to quit the town?
'Twas in the dales thou won'st renown;
I would not, John! for half-a-crown
    Have left thee there;
Taking my lonely journey down
    To rural air.

Needless and perhaps sad to say, Clare never took up Charles Elton's generous invitation. He was but one of many subsequent poets who had a longing to give something to Clare – to really give him friendship, comfort, happiness, understanding – anything within their power. Sir Charles Elton was a bookish Whig and not a bit like the Duke who gave Robert Bloomfield a shilling a day.

Lacewing moth

JOHN CONSTABLE AND JOHN CLARE

I have lived most of life in or near the Stour Valley, and in what is popularly known as the Constable Country. The artist himself heard it described as such. He was travelling in the Blue Coach from Ipswich when a fellow passenger responded to his remark on its beauty, 'Yes, sir, this is Constable's country', unaware of who was seated opposite. The river had been straightened out somewhat and canalised by his father and a catchment committee, and was busy and workaday, yet made even lovelier by the activity which was taking place on its banks, even if nobody wanted such scenes on their walls. Its modest breadth had divided what became Suffolk and Essex since time immemorial. No one owns a river and rarely does anyone change their name. There are a number of Stours – and a Stura in Italy. Stour/Stura – a strong, powerful river. Ours hides these qualities and trails along from Cambridgeshire to the North Sea with hardly enough apparent movement to stir a willow. It is enchantingly reflective, an image-maker par-excellence. When we look over bridges it never carries our face away. Pike return our gaze.

The Constables had lived on its territory for centuries, milling, small-farming, shepherding. John, the artist's descendant and myself were friends. We cycled along its lanes and planned to be writer and painter, visited its architecture and were at home. It was quite unlike John Clare's fenland, with its dark cuts and parallel lines, sluices and drains, but even where it was worked somehow lazier. Constable was born in 1776 and Clare in 1793, so there was just these seventeen years between them. Constable in a fine mansion away from the toil, and Clare right into the toil. Whether they knew of each other no one knows. Constable knew poets like Thomson and Bloomfield and liked to quote them on his pictures. He was proud of Bloomfield's *The Farmer's Boy* because it idealised the relationship between master and men and seemed to describe that between his father and his men.

When, the year after Waterloo, old Golding Constable lay dying he demanded to know if he had at any time wronged an employee, if so he would make it right. 'Never', they said. He had inherited Flatford Mill, a farm and much else beside, not because he was heir by convention, but because the uncle who left it to him had seen that he had the physical strength to run them. He was twenty-six. This legacy coincided with what the agricultural historian Lord Ernle called the golden age of English farming and the age which *The Farmer's Boy* successfully celebrated. 26,000 copies sold. Then came the defeat of Napoleon and the end of government subsidy, and the crash. It seemed to have hit John Clare's aristocracy less devastatingly than it did John Constable's squires.

Socially Clare was an oddity, a peasant poet. Very soon 'peasant' would be turned into 'labourer'. Socially, Constable was not a gentleman until, that was, he was voted R.A. Turner came round to tell him. Abram Constable who now ran Flatford Mill wrote happily to his brother, 'A Royal Academician – and a *Gentleman*!' I could go on fancifully knitting the lives of this great poet and this great painter together, but my reason for making any link at all is because, hunting through my art shelves and finding the glossy reproductions of what a modern critic called 'The ideal countryside of every English mind', I realised for the first time how inhabited it is. Not only the famous scenery, but those who made it, are present. Given second place to Place, certainly, but *there*.

Searching for a possible quote from Clare amongst the many from Bloomfield and Thomson, I found this note by the artist on a picture entitled 'Landscape: Ploughing Scene in Suffolk'. 'I have added some ploughmen to the landscape from the park pale which is a great help, but I must try and warm the picture a little more if I can'. And there, overlooked by me as I, like everyone else, pored over the view, were the men who Clare worked beside. It is a wintry day in the Stour Valley – and in Helpston. The artist admitted it. 'It is bleak and looks as though there would be a shower of sleet, and that you know is too much the case with my things.' And it was too much the case when he painted summer, which he usually did. John Clare, ploughing for the landlord of the Blue Bell, never minded the bleakness. A field was his

At Helpston

notebook. Backwards and forwards, the furrows turned into ruled sheets. Too far off to be wondered at, he filled them up with words. Too far off for me to take them in were the inhabitants of 'my' scenery as I gazed on views.

Constable's peasant-labourers clearly knew their place and seem happy enough in it. Some would have been employed by his family. He was young, tall – 'the handsome miller'. He worked partly in the open air, partly in the cottage-studio at East Bergholt, and then in Soho. Painting by the Stour, he packed-up when the evening meal smoke rose from village chimneys. The locals worked, idled, gossiped, sometime dozed on a bank, and eventually off-palette, as it were, starved. The rural idyll of art and poetry had run into collapse, as it periodically did, only this time in the Suffolk-Essex countryside with violence. Captain Swing was around. But there are no bonfires or banishments to Botany Bay in a Constable, or in a Clare poem. What there is, earlier on, both in East Bergholt and Helpston, is Enclosure, workhouses, great folk and – labourers. Also sickness. The wordy lives of John Constable and John Clare make painful reading.

The young artist in his father's fields was 'beautiful like a Raphael', someone said, 'and guileless'. 'How I amused my leisure walks', he said, 'picking up little scraps of trees – plants – ferns – distances with my pencil.' In September that year, 1814, further ploughing would have gone on to prepare the ground for the winter wheat, as East Bergholt was following the Norfolk Four Course system in which wheat was sown every four years, and other crops each year until then. These agricultural facts, as common to Helpston as the Stour Valley, having been established in my head, I then discovered Constable's own farming manual, *The Farmer's Boy*. It was this lengthy poem which taught him the 'inclusion' of the fields. Nobody must be left out of the everlasting circle of work and its benign results. Both Constable and his close friend John Fisher were shattered when what they thought of was a God-ordained pattern of existence broke down under the unfairness of it all. The clergy and gentry of the Stour Valley fled the unnatural disorder, the rioting, the fires, the terror. The artist heard from Fisher that 'I am too much pulled down by agricultural distress' to buy paintings. He and his uncle were the only buyers of a Constable.

John Constable and John Clare

Clare's father ended his life in the utmost poverty, arthritic and close to the workhouse. Five shillings a long working week, chipping stones by the roadside. Constable's father died in 1816, with his artist son by his side. John then left the room and wandered about in the nearby fields, where he found an abandoned shepherd's hut. He made a pencil drawing of it. John Clare too found an abandoned shepherd's hut and wrote this:

> The Shepherds vanished all and disregard
> Left their old music like a vagrant bee
> For Summer's breeze to murmur o'er and die,
> And these ancient spots mine ear and eye
> Turn listeners till the very wind prolongs
> The theme as wishing in its depth of joy
> To recollect the music of old songs
> And meet the hut that blessed me when a boy.

These huts at this time were similar to children's dens, hay and leaves spread over branches. The shepherd contrived them by each shifting fold as he pastured his sheep across the countryside. Eventually his hut grew iron wheels, and a horse drew it from stop to stop. Roger Deakin had one in his meadow and we used to chat in it. Sometimes in the summer he would sleep in it with the door wide open. Every so often the unseen Norwich train would roar through Roger's acres making a brief turmoil. Clare's shepherds existed on the edge of things on unenclosed land, as did his gypsies. Both travelled on ancient tracks away from habitation.

The footpaths in a Constable are scuffed and well-trodden, the river buildings dank and workaday. His friend Archdeacon Fisher wrote, 'I was the other day fishing in the New Forest in a fine, deep, broad river, with mills, roaring back-waters, withy beds etc. I thought of you often during the day. I caught two pike, was up to the middle in water-meadows, ate my dinner under a willow, and was as happy as when I was a "careless boy".' To which the artist made his now famous apologia.

At Helpston

Old rotten banks, slimy posts and brickwork, I love such things ... They have always been my delight ... I should paint my own places best ... Painting is but another word for feeling. I associate *my* careless boyhood to all that lies on the banks of the *Stour*. They made me a painter.

John Clare's river is precarious, like his life. Some of its springs are stopped-up by Enclosure, as were the sources of his happiness.

> On Lolham Brigs in wild and lonely mood
> I've seen the winter floods their gambols play.
> Through each old arch that trembled as I stood
> Bent o'er the wall to watch the dashing spray
> As their old stations would be washed away.
> Crash came the ice against the jambs and then
> A shudder jarred the arches – yet once more
> It breasted raving waves and stood agen
> To wait the shock as stubborn as before.
> White foam brown-crested with the russet soil,
> As washed from new ploughed lands, would dart beneath,
> Then round and round a thousand eddies boil.

Constable's Flatford Mill, with its race and locks, still spells danger. When he told his brother Abram that he intended to bring his young family there for an autumn holiday after the harvest, there was consternation. Abram wrote that there was no surer way of getting it drowned. However, all went well. And the many boys and girls in the pictures do not look in peril. As a little boy I could hardly bring myself to cross what we called the floodgates where the river became a torrent below a rusty mattress-like bar, so loud that it drowned our shouts.

Part of the water-table of the Stour rises in my garden. How John Clare mourned Enclosure's blocking of the Helpston, or rather the covering over of its wetlands.

> The silver springs, grown naked dykes
> Scarce own a bunch of rushes.
> When grain got high the tasteless tykes

> Grubbed-up trees, banks and bushes.
> And me, they turned me inside out
> For sand and grit and stones
> And turned my old green hills about
> And picked my very bones.

Robert Bloomfield was as much John Constable's perfect village voice as he was Clare's. Under one of the artist's revolutionary cloud studies he quote's *The Farmer's Boy*: 'He views the white-rob'd clouds in clusters driven, and all the glorious pageantry of heaven'. Peasants look up as well as down, are visionary as well as low. Clare looks up all the time, even when he is at the plough. He does not use worn-out imagery when he sees a skylark soaring

> O'er her half-formed nest with happy wings
> Winnows the air – till in the clouds she sings.
> Then hangs, a dust-spot in the sunny skies,
> And drops and drops till in the nest she lies.

This is marvellous. Ornithology, botany, natural history, correct observation have made their way into poetry. But John Constable too, in his London lectures on landscape, explains the scientific basis of his art. But it was not what was wanted. 'It will be difficult to name a class of landscape in which the sky is not the key-note', he said, 'the standard of scale, and the chief Organ of Sentiment ... it governs everything.' But a fellow artist invited him to lie under a tree and simply look up. 'You see, my dear Constable, it is all glazing, all glazing ...'

Constable's celebrity and Clare's fame were brief and close. In 1824 *The Hay Wain* received the Gold Medal at the Paris Salon (and would be a pointer to Impressionism), and in 1820 *Poems Descriptive of Rural Life and Scenery* would be a nine days' wonder (and point towards Ted Hughes, Seamus Heaney and Richard Mabey, amongst many other poets and naturalists.)

No berries and very little leaves left, 2000

THREE UNDERSTANDINGS

Homage poems are usually higher in praise than in real comprehension. Clare has always attracted them. An early and good one was Sidney Keyes' *A Garland for John Clare* and I re-read it still with gratitude. Keyes died in the Western Desert fighting in April 1945. He was not quite twenty-one. With Keith Douglas, Alun Lewis, R.N. Currey and Timothy Corsellis he was among the best poets of the Second World War.

In 1940 he went up to The Queen's College, Oxford as a history scholar where he met John Heath-Stubbs and was taught by Edmund Blunden. Blunden had taken John Clare's poems with him to the trenches and now a quarter of a century on he would be reading them to another generation. Influenced by Blunden, and on John Clare's birthday, July 13th 1941, Keyes wrote his *Garland*. It is youthful and fresh and beautiful. I read it now and then at Helpston.

Keyes went to Dartford Grammar School, a Tudor foundation rather run-down when my friend Anthony Smith became its headmaster. Its other famous pupil was Mick Jagger. On one of my visits there I met his father, then in his nineties, a tall, quiet retired teacher, originally from Yorkshire where, he once told me, he and other boys used to roll stones on the moor. Anthony Smith revived Dartford Grammar School in a quite amazing way, and his daughter Sarah did her doctorate on Keyes. Very soon there was a Sidney Keyes House and a Mick Jagger House. Both Michael Meyer, Keyes' editor, and John Heath-Stubbs his great influence at Oxford, and now blind, and myself, gave lectures on him at Dartford in which Clare was never far off.

A Garland for John Clare

Whether the cold eye and the failing hand
Of these defrauded years ...

At Helpston

    Whether the two-way heart, the laughter
    At little things would please you, John; the waiting
    For louder nightingales, for the first flash and thunder
    Of our awakening would frighten you –
    I wonder sometimes, wishing for your company
    This summer; watching time's contempt
    For such as you and I, the daily progress
    Of couch-grass on a wall, avid as death.
    But you had courage. Facing the open fields
    Of immortality, you drove your coulter
    Strongly and sang, not marking how the soil
    Closed its cut grin behind you, nor in front
    The jealousy of stones and a low sky.
    Perhaps, then, you'll accept my awkward homage –
    Even this backyard garland I have made.

            II

    I'd give you wild flowers for decking
    Your memory, those few I know:
    Far-sighted catseye that so soon turns blind
    And pallid after picking; the elder's curdled flowers,
    That wastrel witch-tree; toadflax crouching
    Under a wall; and even the unpersistent
    Windflowers that wilt to rags within an hour ...
    These for a token. But I'd give you other
    More private presents, as those evenings
    When under lime-trees of an earlier summer
    We'd sing at nine o'clock, small wineglasses
    Set out and glittering; and perhaps my friend
    Would play on a pipe, competing with the crickets –
    My lady Greensleeves, fickle as fine weather
    Or the lighter-boy who loved a merchant's girl.
    Then we would talk, or perhaps silently
    Watch the night coming.
    Those evenings were yours, John, more than mine.

Three Understandings

And I would give you books you never had;
The valley of the Loire under its pinewoods;
My friend Tom Staveley; the carved stone bridge
At Yalding; and perhaps a girl's small face
And hanging hair that are important also.
I'd even give you part in my shared fear;
This personal responsibility
For a whole world's disease that is our nightmare –
You who were never trusted nor obeyed
In anything, and so went mad and died.
We have too much of what you lacked.
Lastly, I'd ask a favour of you, John:
The secret of your singing, of the high
Persons and lovely voices we have lost.
You knew them all. Even despised and digging
Your scant asylum garden, they were with you.
When London's talkers left you, still you'd say
You were the poet, there had only ever been
One poet – Shakespeare, Milton, Byron
And mad John Clare, the single timeless poet.
We have forgotten that. But sometimes I remember
The time that I was Clare, and you unborn.

III

Whether you'd fear the shrillness of my voice,
The hedgehog skin of nerves, the blind desire
For power and safety, that was all my doubt.
It was unjust. Accept, then, my poor scraps
Of proper life, my waste growth of achievement.
Even the cold eye and the failing hand
May be acceptable to one long dead.

In the summer of 1993 to celebrate John Clare's bi-century, R.H. Thomas sent me this. We had met in Ipswich when I chaired his reading in the Town Hall. He was in his eighties and had driven from

At Helpston

Wales. We had supper in a kind of passage restaurant with musak, a solitary couple. He appeared indifferent to this unworthy hospitality and it made me nervous. He stayed a night or two and read at local schools. A forbidding, edgy figure. Then arrived the poem and 'Will this do?' Arguably, it remains the most perceptive modern statement on Clare.

Luna

The moon never sets
in Northampton. Every time
I pass through, it stares
at me from a window
of the asylum and is always
at the full. Don't be misled
by those likenesses of it
when it was new and shone
down on the unenclosed meadows.
As it waxed it became
bald. It was a skull
where names chased one another
without end, wife and sweetheart
hurrying by like shadows
over the corn. For ignorance
time stops by a flower.
Young, he was in his own
sky, rising at mornings
over unbrushed dew.

I used to spend every other Christmas and a week in summer in North Cornwall, where Charles Causley and myself became friends. He lived at 2, Cypress Well, Launceston. He would drive the poet James Turner and myself around on what we called Charles's mystery tour, once to Lew Trenchard to see Baring-Gould's rectory. It had been made an hotel and a wedding was in progress, at which we danced in our rough clothes. It was wild and grey outside. Charles had done his teacher-training in Peterborough, and it was less than an hour on his

Three Understandings

bike to Helpston. He would have been the president of the John Clare Society were it not for the distance. 'Ask Ronnie', he said. Thus it began, the July journey. He had a car by the time he wrote the following.

Helpston

Hills sank like green fleets on the land's long run
About the village of toast-coloured stone.
Leaving the car beside the Blue Bell, we
Walked with a clutch of flowers the clear lane
Towards the grave.

It was well combed, and quiet as before.
An upturned stone boat
Beached at God's thick door.
Only the water in the spiked grave pot
Smelt sourly of death.
Yet no wind seemed to blow
From off the fen or sea.
The flowers flickered in the painted pot
Like green antennae,
As though John Clare from a sounding skull
Brim with a hundred years of dirt and stone
Signalled to us;
And light suddenly breathed
Over the plain.

Later, drinking whisky in the Bull at Peterborough,
The face of the poet
Lying out on the rigid plain
Stared at me
As clearly as it once stared through
The glass coffin-lid
In the church-side pub on his burial day:
Head visible, to prove
The bulging brain was not taken away

At Helpston

    By surgeons, digging through the bone and hair
    As if to find poems still
    Beating there,
    Then, like an anchor, to be lowered fast
    Out of creation's pain, the stropping wind,
    Deep out of sight, into the World's mind.

The grasshopper, Le Lavandou, 1990

JOHN CLARE AND THE PAPER CHASE

It might well have all begun with paper. Lots of fine new paper on which to write. A whole bookful of it. A leather-bound book waiting for words. His publishers had sent it to him, presumably in late summer else, had it arrived at the normal diary time, it would have been half-filled by now. It was a journal without dates, the fifth edition of Taylor and Hessey's *Student's Journal* which they had been issuing for some years. Clare was thrilled with its emptiness, its marbled boards, its timelessness. Inside a note said that it was arranged, printed and ruled for receiving an account of every day's employment for the space of one year. The year John Clare wrote in it was 1824, the month September. Also inside, and to be expected, was a resolution quoted from Mr Gibbons' *Journal*:

> I propose from this day (January 1st) to keep an exact Journal of my Actions and Studies, both to assist my Memory, and to accustom me to set a due value on my Time.

Many years before a friend had sent Gilbert White a similar journal and we know what happened to it. When Taylor and Hessey's present arrived the poet wrote 'John Clare / Helpstone / 1824' on the title-page. The entries, with many omissions, would run from Monday 6 September 1824 to 11 September 1825. His resolution was a rural version of Gibbons':

> I have determind this day of beginning a sort of journal to give my opinion of things I may read or see & set down any thoughts that may arise either in my reading at home or my musings in the Fields

He could have added a record of his state of health and his garden notes, for each of these subjects crop up over and over again. He half-

At Helpston

lived in his cottage garden. He was an avid receiver of plants and seeds, cultivated and wild, with a passion for garden-writing.

But to begin at the beginning, which was more than halfway through the year, 1824 was a time of scarcely believable output. A stream of some of his finest poems, hundreds of letters, essays, starts on stories, an autobiography and the wearing business of his *Shepherd's Calendar*. And this anxiety about paper. Few great writers have been so deprived of this basic material or been so forced to worry about it. Lord Radstock and Mrs Emmerson sent him books and even a waistcoat, but never a ream of paper.

Paper on which to write would be a consideration where poor people were concerned right up until the Second World War. It was rationed in elementary schools. To blot your copy-book was a crime in itself. An army of clerks so revered paper that the ledgers of banks and offices are miracles of penmanship. Classroom inkwells and spluttering nibs were terrifying in case the paper was 'spoilt'. Pencils were a relief but jobs had to be applied for 'in ink'. John Clare sometimes wrote in his copybook hand, and sometimes in such a rough hand that it was near-indecipherable to his modern editors. And of course often on any old paper, crowding the borders and across the creases. Good and bad hands alternate in the *Journal* and there is this constant happy awareness of space, of the fresh page, of the feel of paper. *On* the paper all is not well. Clare's alternating joys and despairs pass across it in immediate confessions, like clouds and brightness crossing a firm sky. The paper belongs to a *Student's Journal* and it has to hold so much mature thought and experience.

Whilst filling it, richly, haphazardly, Clare was waiting for Taylor and Hessey's dragged out decision on the *Shepherd's Calendar,* and was in a sense filling in time. Unbeknown to him they were breaking up and going their own ways. When at long last they sent him proofs his poem was so full of cuts and changes as to be hardly recognisable. If you want to read what Clare wrote and what John Taylor finally published you get a copy of Tim Chilcott's excellent Carcanet edition in which the original text and its altered words stare warily across at each other from opposite pages. We no longer dismiss this heavy handling of Clare, finding it all part of his entrance into literature, but,

John Clare and the Paper Chase

should we ourselves be writers, we feel his hurt and rage. The *Journal* takes us through this not uncommon authorial misery. The proofs begin to arrive in bits and pieces during April 1825, the much changed corrected proofs, that is, and Clare 'Wrote to Hessey in a manner that I am always very loath to write but I could keep my patience no longer.' Hessey wrote back in three days and says, more or less, that if Clare can find a better publisher he can have his manuscripts back. Two months later he gets a letter from Taylor this time to say that 'there is twice as much more as he wants for the *Shepherd's Calenda*r'... Clare calls him 'a very dillatory chap'. Finally, as the *Journal* runs out after further proof alterations of the *Shepherd's Calendar* which rock Clare's own faith in its merit, so does poor John Taylor's health. He has brain fever. Clare, who has recorded his own illness throughout the *Journal* wrote to him warmly. What Tim Chilcott describes as the ambiguity of both Clare and his publisher in the making of this great rural poem is not touched on in the *Student's Journal* but what appears is very grown up. It is as though the poet wants to keep its white pages for better things than the standard rows between author and 'bookseller'. The gift of the Journal itself seems to remind Clare daily of the affection in which it is held. Its entries would move him on into autobiography, into a creativity which he had not suspected. Also, he was/is one of literature's master list-makers and the Journal taught him how important it was to omit nothing. Thus its triumph. So it was as a perpetual learner that he qualified for its ruled entries. Writers are popularly credited with fear of the blank page but Clare saw it as paper in its most delectable form, due to its rarity in his life. An interesting history could be written of basic materials-deprived geniuses. The sculptor Gaudier-Brzeska sneaking forth at midnight to steal scraps of marble from the funerary stonemasons, the rural artist Harry Becker so poor that he could not afford canvas and who had to size sacks on which to paint his wonderful pictures of Suffolk farming. The exquisite patchwork by poor country women could be included in this poverty of working materials. Perhaps there is some record of a well-to-do fan sending John Clare a fat parcel of writing-paper, but I have not read of it. The teenage World War Two poet Sidney Keyes in his *A Garland for John*

At Helpston

Clare wants to give him everything, including 'more private presents', but these do not include paper.

> And I would give you books you never had;
> The valley of the Loire under its pinewoods;
> My friend Tom Staveley; the carved stone bridge
> At Yalding...

... being too young to know, in spite of Edmund Blunden's teaching at Oxford, that Clare was piled high with books, possessed the Nene Valley, was surrounded by friends and in some way owned Lolham Bridge. Although true to say, only for a while.

Clare was sick on and off throughout this diary. It is wretched to read of these unspecified bouts of illness. He is not a person to keep them off the page. Waves of depression, headaches, strangely frightening attacks of this and that. To write them down seems a possible cure. Sympathising, Mrs Emmerson sends him Beresford's *The Miseries of Human Life* 'with the hope that its witty and clever contents may serve to beguile his occasional melancholy hours'. She adds a thoughtful exclamation mark, a kind of cheer-up! But the attacks continue and we know where they are leading, alas. All the same an exciting creative energy runs all through the *Student's Journal*. It belongs to a Clare who is daily learning about himself. Dreary proofs, the jobbery which even a poet must work at, yes, but a veritable ceaseless output of poems, and maybe a life of his hero Robert Bloomfield who had died the year before. But something even more marvellous than all this was 'my intention to call my Natural History of Helpstone "Biographies of Birds and Flowers"'. At last he knew what to do with what lay around the crowded cottage, the noisy pub and the village generally. That glorious area which made him also 'a tenant of the fields' – as he would obituarize a dead farm labourer. But a vital all-seeing tenant – owner even. It was these tumbling over one another plans which were his medicine. The entries telling of his lows and highs are infectious. If only there could be some even keel, one prays, knowing that there could never be. On Wednesday 13 July he writes, 'This day I am thirty-two, or thirty-three, I am not certain which.' And two pretty girls drank his health. Once outside researching his biographies he was a happy eager youth again.

Earlier this year, on 9 March 1825, 'I had a very odd dream last night and I take it as an ill omen for I don't expect that the book will meet a better fate – I thought I had one of the proofs of *The Shepherd's Calendar* from London & after looking at it awhile it shrank thro my hands like sand & crumbled into dust – the birds were singing in Oxey wood at 6 oclock this evening as loud and various as at May.'

This was the time when Clare, the Billings brothers, the brilliant Joseph Henderson and the learned Edmund Artis were able to escape their various domestic duties – not that the Billings ever did much in that line – and to be who they really were, the rural intellectuals. Clare was at work on two books at the same time, one this *Journal*, the other his autobiography. The *Journal* appeared to be a happy or at least a not dreaded task but the autobiography proved hard going. Three years earlier he had sent his publishers a brief account of his existence called *Sketches in the Life of John Clare* but the *Journal* would not see light until Margaret Grainger included it in her splendid *The Natural History Prose Writings of John Clare* in 1983.

Both these books brought me into touch with their editors, Edmund Blunden and Margaret Grainger, and both at Colchester. I had discovered the *Sketches* in a secondhand bookshop, the rare Cobden Sanderson edition of 1931. It was my first glimpse of John Clare. Enthralled, I invited Edmund Blunden to come to our literary society to talk about him. It was our first meeting. After the talk we drank beer in the Red Lion (of course) and then I walked to the station with him, a long way. He was slight, with a bird-like face and movement. As the London train pulled in he gave me his lecture notes. Beautiful writing. I placed them in the *Sketches*, where they still are. For a few years later, after he had moved to Long Melford, close to my birthplace, I would see him sitting in the Bull at eleven a.m. sharp. He lived in a house which Siegfried Sassoon had bought for him. Years earlier he and Sassoon would bicycle around Suffolk and I described this brief acquaintance in talks at Long Melford after his death. I was in my twenties and the John Clare Society was aeons away. Hazlitt would write dizzily about 'My first Acquaintance with Poets' (Coleridge and

At Helpston

Wordsworth), and it is something one is never likely to forget. When Blunden came to Helpston to unveil the plaque on Clare's cottage, Edward Storey took him to the pub, to marvel at his capacity.

Margaret I met for the one and only time, alas, for she was ill, when she came to the Clare Symposium at the Minories in Colchester. My old friend Charles Causley, forever associated with his Clare bicycle tyre poem, came too. And all the way from Cornwall. Fed up with waiting for the traffic to stop in the High Street, he affected a shocking limp and there was a great halt, and over we three crossed like Israelites over the Red Sea. What we all said at the Symposium has vanished into the wordy air. In Cornwall Charles Causley would take me to his secret places and in Suffolk, on his birthday, I took him to see Edward FitzGerald's grave with its rose from Omar Khayyám's tomb in Persia. It was midnight and we shushed each other, fearful of waking the living in the nearby cottages. These fragments have become part of my Clare experience and some of them will be in my old diaries. 'Charles', they will say, 'the Minories 2.30'. In his Launceston he would be a boy again and throw pebbles into the stone Virgin's lap. He hated gardening.

In these midsummer days, with the Festival nigh, I sit in the garden to return to the doubly self-revealing efforts of John Clare in the *Journal* year of September 1824-5, with the *Life* so difficult and the *Biographies* rushing along. It is not uncommon for writers to scribble two books at the same time. The hard one, with Blunden's blessing I have read for ages, the soft and bright as birds' wings one lies on the grass at this moment, too beautiful, like a cake, to be swallowed fast. 'Saw the red start or Firetail to day & little Willow wren – the black thorn tree in full flower that shines about the hedges like cloaths hung out to dry [...] I observed a Snail on his journey at full speed & I marked by my watch that he went 13 Inches in 3 minutes which was the utmost he coud do without stopping to wind or rest it was the large Garden snail.'

Reading on, I note how rarely Clare mentions housework and imagine that, like Charles Darwin, he read and wrote in domestic chaos. He is surprisingly worldly and no fool when it comes to that worst kind of paperwork, answering business letters, making a will etc.

John Clare and the Paper Chase

He is a blunt reviewer but also fresh and startling in his criticism of what he is reading. 'I dislikd Wordsworth because I heard he was dislikd & I was astonishd when I looked into him [...] finding him so natural & beautiful.' Keats 'looked into' Chapman's Homer.

The *Journal* belongs to a born collector. Clare does not come home empty-handed, and Patty would have sighed and the children would have raided his pockets. As an inveterate collector he shocks us by digging up his finds to replant them behind the cottage, crowded as it was one way and another. Did they all root? Take? Could any of them be there now? You never know with flowers.

> Took a walk to Lolham brigs to hunt for a species of fern that usd to grow on some willow tree heads in Lolham lane when I was a boy but coud find none – got some of the yellow water lily [*Nupher lutea*] from the pits which the floods had washd up to set in an old water tub in the garden & to try some on land in a swaily [shady] corner as the horse blob thrives well which is a water flower – listend in the evening to the glinton bells at the top of the garden I always feel mellancholy at this season to hear them & yet it is a pleasure – 'Im pleasd & yet Im sad'

It is November 1st. There he stands, the apples gone for rent, the far ringers practising. He quotes Kirke White's 'When twilight steals along the ground' and one feels a chill in the air. Two days later he walks all the way to Swordy Well with John Billings to gather Old Man's Beard (*Clematis Vitalba*) but sometimes called War in Northamptonshire. They entered Hilly Wood to find Common Brake (bracken), Fox Fern (*Dryopteris filix-mas*) Hart's Tongue (*Phyllitis scolopendrium*) and 'polopody two sorts – the tall & the dwarf'. The autumn world had come right again.

Now and then he is sexy. Hoping that the rain will force the women to pull up their skirts so that he can glimpse their legs, they frustrate him by lowering them to hide their muddy stockings. He himself is good-looking. The huge brow which in later years would crush down on his features – not unlike Darwin's – was wide and handsome and decked with red-gold curls. His adored children run into the pages.

At Helpston

'My dear boy Frederick is one yeer old this day' – 6 January 1825. The reader knows what they do not, the approaching severance. This is the poignancy of the published diary, the blankness of the morrow for the writer, its full entry for the reader.

Clare, as with all villagers, enjoys sensational news and gossip, handing it on to the *Student's Journal* where it gets tangled up with botany and grief, with gloomy meditations on his fate, his burial arrangements, the shortcomings of publishers and his ambition. For he is ambitious and has every right to be so. He knows his worth. This is what makes him so upset when certain folk treat him more as a phenomenon – like one of those oddities who creep into the *Stamford Mercury* and not as a man of letters. 'There is now living at Barton an old lady of the name of Faunt who has nearly attained the great age of 105 years – she has lately cut *new teeth* to the great supprise of the family.' Thomas Hardy would cut out news like this from the Dorset papers all his life. One never knew when they might come in handy.

On 1 February 1825 John Clare thought that he might solve the paper problem. 'A beautiful morning took a walk in the fields saw some birch poles in the quick fencing & fancyd the bark of birch might make a good substitute for Paper. It is easily parted in thin lairs [layers] & one shred of bark round the tree woud split into 10 or a dozen sheets & I have tryd it & find it recieves the ink very readily.' Whilst writing *The Woodlanders* and taking a break where the real women were working, Hardy would have a sudden inspiration and would pencil it down on a chip, often stuffing his pockets with these white sappy notes as thought after thought occurred to him. Clare would use his hard hat as a desk. Paper-hunger would follow to the grave.

Dreadful things went on. Had there not been this need to find something to say in a diary we might never have heard of them. Things which cast a grim light on human nature. It would have been Clare the archaeologist who felt it necessary to record the following. It showed how noble things vanished. Not in wind and weather but most likely as patch for the bodger.

Sunday 6 March 1825
Parish Officers are modern Savages as the following fact will testifye – Crowland Abbey – 'Certain surveyors have lately dug up several foundation stones of the Abby and also a great quantity of stone coffins for the purpose of repairing the parish roads!!'
Stamford Mercury

A similar fate overtook the medieval images in a Suffolk church near me. It stood in a farmyard and a Georgian farmer crumbled them up and mended his track with them. It was Clare the archaeologist speaking. Whether it was an old stile, an ancient tree, a filled-in brook or the ignorant use of a Roman site, he waged battle against their destroyers. Not in the *Journal* but unforgettably he says, 'The heathen mythology is fond of indul[g]ing in the metramorp[h]ing of the memory of lovers & heroes into the births of flowers & I coud almost fancy that this blue anenonie sprang from the blood or dust of the romans for it [only] haunts [two places] the roman bank in this neighbourhood [and] the roman bank agen Burghley Park'. This would have gone into his *Biographies of Birds and Flowers* had that masterpiece been completed. Clare's classicism often suits the Greek and Roman legends more than that of those who read Classics. The old earthiness has not been shaken out from it. He went on three kind of gigs, as a labourer, as a plant collector and as a trained – by Mr Artis – archaeologist.

Family life doesn't get much of a look in where the *Journal* is concerned and when it does I find myself clutching at it greedily. He shares his house not only with six other humans but with rats. Everyone did. He would listen to them having 'a terrible kick up [...] in the cieling'. And sometimes 'all thro last night' he heard 'the sort of watch ticking noise calld a death watch [beetle] & observed there was one on each side [of] the chamber & as soon as one ceased ticking the other began I think it is a call that the male & female use in the time of cohabiting.' He saw Patty lying there listening. Outside the stone chippings which his crippled father made for five shillings a week would fly about as the early morning carts lumbered beneath their window.

At Helpston

> Friday 6 May 1825
> Coud not sleep all night got up at three oclock in the morning & walkd about the fields – the birds were high in their songs in Royce wood & almost deafning […] saw a Hawk like bird that made an odd noise like one of the notes of the Nightingale as if to decoy his prey

One way and another the poet himself, a wild spirit, was being decoyed to Epping, to Northampton, to the safe houses of his day.

Swan and alders

EDMUND BLUNDEN AND JOHN CLARE

Address given in Long Melford Church, Suffolk, on the centenary of Blunden's birth, 1996.

Poets have their own way of keeping in touch with one another, and it is always unexpected. At the outbreak of World War Two it was popularly expected that its poets would instantly reach out their hands to the poets of the Great War, as it was called, to Wilfred Owen, Siegfried Sassoon, Rupert Brooke – and Edmund Blunden. But instead, and to the mystification of many of their readers, they held out their hands to Hölderlin and Rilke, two German poets of whom the public knew little or nothing.

We are here today for myriad reasons which time has drawn together to remember Edmund Blunden's birth just a hundred years ago, and to not forget that he was the twenty-three year old who first shook the dust of forgetfulness from the bright poet who for so long lay incarcerated in Peterborough Museum, and to remind ourselves that it was the youthful Blunden who in a sense became our Clare after the Armistice, giving a voice to poor rural Suffolk when he and his wife lived near here at Stansfield.

I knew him slightly when I was young. He was then retired to the Mill House, Long Melford, given to him by Siegfried Sassoon. The mill ford from which this huge grand village takes its name laps its walls. Edmund was a small, quick, bird-like man, bookish, widely travelled yet deeply rooted in both Kent and Suffolk. I remember a long walk to Colchester Station with him and his quick gaze at the grim building inscribed 'North-East Essex Lunatic Asylum' as we climbed to the booking office, and his giving me a bundle of lecture notes in his beautiful hand just as the train puffed in. This when I myself had just begun to write. Later, we would discover him at midday in the Bull at Long Melford and talk shop.

At Helpston

On John Clare's centenary in 1964 Blunden gave a lecture at the Aldeburgh Festival describing how 'this great writer' was 'revived in 1919' by himself and a fellow undergraduate Alan Porter, which was as loving an act in literature as can be found. In 1919 Edmund Blunden took up the Oxford Scholarship which he had been awarded in 1914, but had postponed because of the war. No sooner had he settled in than he and Alan Porter decided that 'Clare was a neglected but entrancing poet, and before long we had almost signed in our blood a pact that we would not cease from mental strife, and so on, until we had built Clare's scattered poetry up again, the unknown with the known'. As Alan Porter was destined to be an English professor at Vassar, he might now be rightly thought of as the founder of Clare studies in the U.S.A., for it is hardly likely that such an enthusiast would not have led the Michigan girls to the poet, among them the recently arrived Edna St Vincent Millay.

Blunden's and Porter's first call was on aged Dr Druce the Oxford botanist, who had actually seen John Clare, 'a solitary looking at the sky', as he said. He lived in Crick Road and his letter of introduction unlocked the Peterborough cupboards for these eager young friends, who rushed around Helpston with no preparation and scarcely any money, finding the grave, the birthplace, the monument and, in the city, more poetry than could have ever been imagined. At Aldeburgh Blunden said that Clare had been neglected because the world never knew the half of him. But how could such a writer have remained so fragmented, so lost, for so long? Blunden had come to John Clare whilst still a boy via a now little remembered but excellent writer named Arthur Symonds. In 1908 at the age of twelve he came across Symonds's selection of Clare's work in the Oxford Library of Prose and Poetry, made at the time when Symonds himself was suffering from mental illness, thus bringing him near to Clare in a deeply personal sense. Symonds had known Verlaine and Mallarmé, and had anticipated Calvino with a delightful book called *Cities*. He too, like Blunden, lived in Kent, thus we enter the literary labyrinth in whose rich corridors writers cross paths, time and experiences.

Edmund Blunden took his Arthur Symonds selection of John Clare to the Western Front. It was the tradition of many soldiers to carry a pocket edition of their favourite book all through the war. Blunden tells in *Undertones of War*, published ten years after the Armistice, how he lost his Clare. His troop had been sent to some huts in a cherry orchard to learn gas-drill. While this went on the officers sat around talking poetry. They were three kilometres from the line. The cherry orchard was filled with convolvulus, linnets, butterflies, even if the young soldiers were forced to run through the gas-filled huts with flannel masks over their heads. With Blunden was an officer friend named Xavier Kapp, later the famous cartoonist. It was he who stole his Clare. Blunden wrote:

> I will stay in this farmhouse while the gas course lasts and to get the old peasant in the evenings to recite more La Fontaine to me in the Bethune dialect! and read – Bless me, Kapp has gone away with my John Clare! He has the book yet for all I know!'

In 1917 many previously reserved occupations, including farmworkers, were called up. The Third Ypres, or Passchendaele was due. Blunden ends his *Undertones of War* with ironic references to the labour corps digging the Haig Line and himself in tours of inspection, not only of his poor men but of 'the willows and waters which are so silvery and unsubstantial' that one could spend a lifetime painting them. He watched his countrymen and rejoiced that at that moment anyway 'No destined anguish lifted its snaky head to poison a harmless young shepherd in a soldier's coat.'

After Oxford Blunden rented a cottage near Clare, Suffolk. He too was a young man who gazed on the countryside with a clear eye. It is now 1922 and he has done much work on the rehabilitation of John Clare, bringing together the known and the unknown, and himself finding out who this astonishing writer really was as he continues to smooth out the manuscripts at Peterborough, touching his pages, getting the drift of his pencil. Siegfried Sassoon is about to arrive at Clare Station and Blunden goes to meet him. From Sassoon's diary:

> 16 June 1922. I left here early on Monday morning, and reached Clare station about 12.30.... It was a sunshiny day, and there was little

At Helpston

Blunden waiting for me in his shabby blue suit. He had just picked up a first edition of *Atalanta in Calydon* for a shilling in a little shop in Clare. And outside the station sat Mary B. in a smart blue cloak, in a tiny wagonette drawn by a small white pony. (A conveyance hired from a farmer and driven by his juvenile daughter.) Slowly we traversed the four miles to Stansfield, up and down little hills among acres of beans and wheat. Arrived at Belle Vue, a stone-faced slate-roofed box of a house by the roadside. And for three days B. and I talked about county cricket and the war and English poetry and East Anglia and our contemporaries ... And I read Clare and Bloomfield and Blunden. And the weather became chilly and it rained on Tuesday and Wednesday; and we drank port by a small fire after dinner. And B. hopped about the house in his bird-like way; and we both received a letter from 'old Hardy' by the same post. And we admired the old man's calligraphy. And we bicycled to Sudbury and lost our road home and had to push the machines across three wheat-fields.

An anthology entitled *Poetry of the Year, or Pastorals from our Poets Illustrative of the Seasons*, with pictures by Birket Foster and David Cox, and published in 1867, just three years after Clare's death, placed him more or less where he would stay until Arthur Symonds and then Blunden rescued him. It contains four poems by him, all of them altered, one bowdlerised. By what can only be a strange coincidence, the collection is opened with those lines from Thomson's *Seasons* which Clare read as a child and which, he said, decided him to be a poet. Among the contributors are Chatterton, Crabbe, Shakespeare, Herrick, Gray, Burns, Keats and Bloomfield, so good company. Even among these Clare's voice is strong and distinctive, and clearly saying far more than what is on a pretty page.

In 1931 Blunden published for the first time *Sketches in the Life of John Clare by Himself*. Blunden was now teaching at Oxford after a spell in Tokyo and had discovered enough about John Clare to spread his name wherever he went. What thrilled him was his accuracy and his power to sing the almost unchanged realities and imaginings of the village, for in Blunden's time whether in Kent or Suffolk, 'Helpston' was just up the road. Nor was it far from Acton, my own Suffolk birthplace three miles from Long Melford, where he came to rest. The farms were in a kind of turmoil during the Twenties and Thirties as the great agricultural depression, briefly lifted by subsidies during the first world war, came down on the fields like the proverbial wet blanket. I glimpsed it from a tall old thatched house lit by oil-lamps and candles, and watered by a pond and a well. Plough-horses jingled and snorted in the yard and when the crops demanded it, hoards of itinerant workers appeared to do pea-picking and similar tasks, many of the young men wearing bits of khaki. The wild flowers were glorious. By the end of summer the Stour was so filled with them in places that we could not see the river at all. Only the road fields were cared for. What lay behind them was our boyhood paradise, all the riches of poverty and neglect. Blunden's love of Clare had a lot to do with his gratitude for 'coming through', as the war survivors described it, and with his conviction that although Clare 'could not but report freshly, in his own pleasant vocabulary, upon the life and environment of a village labourer in the days of George lV' what he said remained both excitingly and sadly valid in the post-armistice England of George V. In his poem *East Anglia* Blunden catches at the hardness which keeps rural life ticking, no matter what:

> In a frosty sunset
>   So fiery red with cold
> The footballers' onset
>   Rings out glad and bold;
> Then boys from daily tether
>   With famous dogs at heel
> In starlight meet – together
>   And to farther hedges steal;
> Where the rats are pattering
>   In and out the stacks,
> Owls with hatred chattering
>   Swoop at the terriers' backs
> And, frost forgot, the chase grows hot
>   Till a rat's a foolish prize,
> But the cornered weasel stands his ground,

At Helpston

> Shrieks at the dogs and boys set round,
> Shrieks as he knows they stand all around,
> And hard as winter dies.

When Blunden was finding Clare there was no sign of the second agricultural revolution to come. Only a second war would hustle it into existence. He saw the bankrupt farmers selling up, holding furious protests on Newmarket heath, refusing any longer to pay tithes to the Church of England, and amidst all the clamour the particular quiet of poverty. He was in fact seeing the slow-vanishing of 'Helpston' though neither he nor any of us knew it. What he witnessed was hedgers and ditchers digging the trenches and horsemen from the farms ploughing their way through the mud in Flanders, and the white war memorials going up in every village, and what he discovered was an inventory of such people for too long locked away at Peterborough which sang their praises and told who and what they really were.

Bullfinch inside a bush, 1984

THE ULTIMATE DIVIDE

As most people did during the early nineteenth century, John Clare possessed a voice for those who could read and write, and for those who could not. We find in him no condemnation of illiteracy but a ferocious condemnation of 'clowns', that Shakespearian term for rustic fools. What riled Clare was their downright refusal to see what lay before their eyes and which did not require learning to identify it, a flower, a bird, any sight which carried with it feeling and intelligence. For such proudly ignorant neighbours he had nothing but rage. It was they who brought the peasantry into common mockery and who created its stereotypes. He also felt that nature demanded an understanding, a worship even, of those whose lives were closest to it. To turn away from any kind of comprehension of what surrounded the village was to him perverse and, worse, destructive. Violence and savagery could drive the plough. Could indeed drive men like himself out. Clowns existed in every class, shedding their blindness in all directions. Whether they were literate or not never came into it. Clare divided his time between well-read friends such as Edmund Artis and Joseph Henderson, household steward and head gardener respectively to Lord Milton, plus distinguished antiquarian and botanist to the neighbourhood, and to un-read companions such as the gypsies, the herdboys and the lads and girls in the inns, and his own family, father, mother and wife. He believed that the brutality of the countryside continued to persist because the loveliness of plants was ignored, animals were killed as a matter of course and the marvels of the universe deliberately turned into an unread book.

When, later in the nineteenth century, Thomas Hardy gave village people intelligent, even profound voices, his novel-reading public was bewildered. A few decades earlier Jane Austen had forced her heroine Emma to recognise that a young farmer could write a good letter, thus disturbing the educated and non-educated division of the countryside

At Helpston

which so conveniently existed then. Literacy and non-literacy was more complex than imagined. Clare's mother and wife were illiterate yet clearly not ignorant, and we have only to glance at the little vestry at Glinton to realise that only a handful of local children could have learnt their letters in it. The very fact of their being sent to school would have set them apart. And we come to the mystery of the unlettered — that not being able to read and write gave them a different intelligence, not 'ignorance'. The literate cannot know what they have lost or the illiterate what they might have gained. I knew quite a number of neighbours who could not read and write in the Suffolk countryside when I was a boy, and I longed to find what they could 'see', that they 'knew', – their heads empty of 'reading' – and full of something else, they usually being so eloquent and differently intelligent. The normality of the many illiterate and the few who could read and write in Helpston made two cultures. Had Clare been one of those farmworkers who could read the Bible and the Peterborough newspaper, his fellows would have admired him and used his skill on the few occasions when they needed to make their mark. But he overstepped the mark. The ceaseless nose-in-a-book business was an affront to them. 'Who did he think he was', etc. He felt his situation, often painfully, and there were those who would have rescued him from it and placed him where everyone read and wrote, unable to comprehend that this village, and none other, was his power base. It was obvious to those who knew him at 'proper' work that books sapped his strength. He had a reputation for sneaking off, for getting out of tasks, for laziness – the worst kind of reputation one could have, man or woman – child even. Worse, they couldn't know what he wrote about them, so they felt exposed by him, which wasn't 'right'. In any case what was there in Helpston for him to be forever putting down on paper? And why didn't his head burst from so much reading? Until recently Dr Fenwick Skrimshire's verdict on the main cause of Clare's insanity, 'after years addicted to poetical prosing', has been seen as an ignorant, even a Philistine one. But Jonathan Bate is surely correct in seeing it as containing some accuracy. For years the poet's friends had noticed the nervous excitement which accompanied his composition and felt worried about it. Illiterate country people, vigorous and

The Ultimate Divide

intelligent in their own sphere, would until quite recently equate book-reading with ill health. As for book-writing, this would produce less wonder than fear, and was as Clare said his mother believed, among the 'black arts'.

Once, during the process of reviewing Wordsworth's *The Excursion*, William Hazlitt sat in a Wiltshire inn, reading and making notes. And drinking. In this poem there is a passage about the kind of rustic literacy which knows its place and does not stray into 'literature'. It describes a young Scottish herdsman who, although he had attended his stepfather's school, 'had small need of books' once he had discovered Nature. Indeed he was one of:

> the poets that are sown
> By Nature! When endow'd with highest gifts –
> The vision, and the faculty divine –
> yet wanting the accomplishment of Verse ...

One day this young man walks to the nearest town:

> He duly went with what small overplus
> His earnings might supply, and brought away
> The book which most had tempted his desires
> While at the stall he read. ...

No, it wasn't James Thomson's *The Seasons*, but 'the divine Milton', and this single book sufficed him for the rest of his long life. Whatever other learning he had came from Lakeland scenery and the stars. Wordsworth encountered him on his long walks, a poet who could but did not write. Hazlitt was reading about him in the Wiltshire pub when he heard it—the jeer, the irrepressible mockery of John Clare's 'clowns', and thus there arrived what is probably the most furious tirade against rural ignorance in English literature.

> Ignorance is always bad enough; but rustic ignorance is intolerable ... The benefits of knowledge are never so well understood as from seeing the effects of ignorance, in their naked, undisguised state,

upon the common country people. Their selfishness and insensibility are perhaps less owing to the hardships and privations, which make them, like people out at sea in a boat, ready to devour one another, than to their having no idea of anything beyond themselves and their immediate sphere of action. They have no knowledge of, and consequently can take no interest in, anything which is not an object of their senses, and of their daily pursuits. They hate all strangers, and have generally a nick-name for the inhabitants of the next village ... The common people in civilised countries are a kind of domesticated savages.

This in 1817, the year before Clare was lime-burning at Casterton and lying low in the fields in his spare time to write and write, and read and read, and to stay out of his people's sight, and to qualify at the vast university of nature.

The solace which writers commonly share is reading. Theirs is a special entrée to literature. They enter the pages of those who created them in a unique way and find themselves at home. It was his reading which both anchored Clare and at the same time sent him off on journeys which took him away from local boundaries. Writers read unmethodically, obscurely, popularly as well as scholarly. Their bookshelves can come as a shock to their readers, for they are a muddle of the haphazard and the expected. Hazlitt remained loyal to any writer, good or bad, who had given him pleasure, even when he had outgrown them.

Due to the circumstances of Clare's life his books tended to be only of the best. He was in a sense an extension of the literate villager with his *Bible, Book of Common Prayer* and *Pilgrim's Progress* who read little else. After the success of his *Poems Descriptive of Rural Life and Scenery* in 1820, books rained in on him from every quarter and even Sidney Keyes, an Oxford undergraduate celebrating Clare's birthday on 13 July 1941, cries, 'I would give you books you never had', not knowing that in this respect the poet was rich. Lord Radstock gave him sermons, of course. It was inevitable. And, equally inescapable, from Mrs Emmerson arrived Young's *Night Thoughts*. Lord Milton gave him Crabbe, Dryden, Goldsmith, Pope, until callers became startled by the contrast between the poverty of his cottage and the wealth of its shelves. John Clare's most methodological read took place at Milton Hall where he studied for the great work that never was, his *Natural History of Helpstone*. There, Margaret Grainger believed, he might have read Thomas Bewick's *A General History of Quadrupeds*, William Curtis's *Botanical Magazine*, Donovan's *Natural History of Insects*, William Hayes's *Natural History of British Birds*, and of course Gilbert White's *Selborne*. All these books were included in the Sothebys' sale from Milton Hall library in 1918. What pleased John Clare most as he thought about his publishers' suggestion that he might join the natural history authors was a recent title on their list, *Flora Domestica or the portable Flower-garden* by Elizabeth Kent, for in it she had written, 'None have better understood the language of flowers than the simple-minded peasant-poet, Clare, whose volumes are like a beautiful country, diversified with woods, meadows, heaths and flower-gardens ... This poet is truly a lover of Nature: in her humblest attire she still is pleasing to him, and the sight of a simple weed seems to him a source of delight. In his lines to Cowper Green, he celebrates plants that seldom find a bard to sing them.' Margaret Grainger says that Elizabeth Kent and Clare approach flowers in a remarkably similar way, communicating an infectious delight in plants to their readers. Both have reservations about Linnaean classification. Clare says 'the hard nicknaming system of unutterable words now in vogue only overloads it in mystery till it makes darkness visible'. But, he adds, since his Natural History must be correct he will ask Mr Henderson, the Milton Hall head gardener and his friend, to check the necessary classification of the plants he will mention. Thus the ambitious project began, the poet reading his head off and now for the first time not hiding away to do it, but asking everyone in Helpston to tell him their stories about bird, beast, plant, weather and insect. And what tales came from them! His notion of them as clowns must have taken a knock. Better managed by Taylor and Hessey, who knows what might not have happened? Pressurised in this venture, as in all the rest, the vulnerable mechanism broke. It takes time for a writer to read himself into a new book.

At Helpston

We might now come to that little booklist which Clare felt obliged to send his publishers in 1822 to show how well-read he was. They had sent him John Keats's own copy of Chaucer – on loan it was. In it Clare read *The Flower and the Leaf* which the nightingale sings. Also *The Complaint of the Black Knight*. He lies on the ground all pale and wan due to his girl's unkindness. As for the author of *La Belle Dame sans Merci*, he was on his way to Italy, Taylor and Hessey having helped to pay his fare. Clare loved Keats's Chaucer. Chaucer was on the list of his favourite poets who 'went to Nature for their images'. Among them was Spenser, Cowley's *The Swallow*, in which the poet accuses the bird at his bedroom window of interrupting his dream, a dream which happened to be better than any reality, including that of the swallow, Shakespeare, Milton's *L'Allegro* and *Il Penseroso* and *Comus*, all three of which Wordsworth's one-book countryman would have read over and over again, then John Gay's *The Shepherd's Week*, in which, on Friday we have a girl's funeral:

> With wicker rods we fenc'd her tomb around
> To ward from man and beast the hallow'd ground.

By the side of the busy road at Kentford, near Newmarket, lies the grave of a shepherd or gypsy lad similarly protected by 'wicker' (willow) rods to this day. Clare's list continues with Matthew Green's *The Spleen* (1737), a witty affair. Green worked in the City of London where they tried to prosecute him for feeding the cats. He wrote his defence as a poem – and was allowed to continue giving them milk. Close to *The Spleen* comes William Collins's *Ode to Evening*, which would have spoken all too plainly to a tired walker on the Barnack road:

> Now air is hushed, save where the weak-eyed bat
> With short shrill shriek flits by on leathern wing ...

Collins, Christopher Smart and John Clare all shared the fate of what in their day was called 'the overthrow of the mind', yet the last of these, I have always believed, went to his books for recovery. He possessed two copies of Gray's poems at Northampton asylum. Thomas Gray, George Crabbe and Clare himself all spoke up for the least regarded yet most essential of toilers:

> Some village Hampden that with dauntless breast
> The little tyrant of his fields withstood ...

It was Admiral Lord Radstock who gave Clare one of his most loved poets, William Cowper. Radstock had written a book called *The Cottager's Friend*. Clare liked what he called 'the bluntness and open heartedness of the sailor', the shabby clothes and the Admiral's indifference to whether he offended or pleased.

Writers do not retreat into books, they advance. They meet their equals, their betters, their inferiors, but rarely know where they themselves stand. All they know is that they are in good company – the best that they are likely to find. To enter a book is to escape from a prison or an emptiness. John Clare carried around with him his twin freedoms, his inventory of Helpston as he had known it in his youth – and his library. The latter included Wordsworth's *Miscellaneous Poems*, 1820, given to him by his father Parker, and his Robert Bloomfield, a writer he thought of as a brother. At the end of Clare's book-list we read why he made it – as a CV to show his fitness to write 'What I intend to call my Natural History of Helpstone "Biographies of Birds and Flowers", with an Appendix on Animals & Insects'. And when he corresponds with Taylor and Hessey in order to create the wonderful natural history that never was, we discover a fine integration of wide reading and specialist reading, and a new kind of authority where this subject is concerned. A chronic addiction to books marries, as it were, the trained eye. What Clare saw in his countryside and what he read in it come together.

Here we have John Clare speaking up for those who were able to see only, who had vision but not literacy:

> Many are poets, though they use no pen
> To show their labours to the snuffling age.
> Real poets must be truly honest men

At Helpston

    Tied to no mongrel laws on flattering page.
    No zeal have they for wrong, or party rage.
    The life of labour is a rural song
    That hurts no cause, nor warfare tries to wage.
    Toil, like the brook, in music wears along.
    Great little minds claim right to act the wrong.

Sheep packing into the barn for food

JOHN CLARE AND THE GYPSIES

Sometimes I watch a film or read a book, come-to and tell myself, 'But I was there! I heard it, I saw it.' It is a not uncommon experience. It occurs when I read John Clare on the gypsies. He both hobnobbed with them and was fastidious where they were concerned, was prejudiced and unprejudiced at the same time. He wrote many poems about them which envied their lot, their freedom, their women, and one poem which envied them nothing.

> The snow falls deep; the Forest lies alone:
> The boy goes hasty for his load of brakes,
> Then thinks upon the fire and hurries back;
> The Gipsy knocks his hands and tucks them up,
> And seeks his squalid camp, half hid in snow,
> Beneath the oak, which breaks away the wind,
> And bushes close, with snow like hovel warm:
> There stinking mutton roasts upon the coals,
> And the half-roasted dog squats close and ribs,
> Then feels the heat too strong and goes aloof;
> He watches well, but none a bit can spare.
> And vainly waits the morsel thrown away:
> 'Tis thus they live – a picture to the place;
> A quiet, pilfering, unprotected race.

It is masterly in its realism. Though one observation would not be ours – 'a picture to the place'. Today's Travellers' encampment has swapped the vardo for the mobile home, horses for horse-power and horse-dealing for scrap metal, and is anathema in our twinked countryside. We, the council, intended the Traveller (is 'gypsy' P.C.? – or not? – it is all rather worrying) to just winter on the official site, then push on, not to purchase them and turn them into messy caravan

At Helpston

additions to our village. We like the gypsies best at the horse-fairs, when they return to being their colourful selves, painted wagons, fortune-tellers, dark-eyed beauties, lively yearlings and all. Appleby Fair is where they should be. No scrap-dealing there.

I was a churchwarden of St Peter's Charsfield, Suffolk, when I was writing *Akenfield*. It was the mid-Sixties, a moment of seismic change in East Anglia as all over the countryside, although, like everyone else, I had no notion of it. One afternoon I found Mr King, our gravedigger for miles around, throwing up clay by the churchyard hedge. He was one of those not uncommon men who would hold back on some subjects and hold forth on others, being what we called 'contrary'. You could never be certain whether he would tell you everything or nothing. Thus,

'Whose grave is it, Mr King?'
'Never you mind. You wouldn't know her.'
'Her?'
'No-one you would know.'
'When is the funeral then?'
'Friday they reckon.'

Dig, dig, dig. Then, seeing my still inquisitive face from down below, he said, 'Ocean'.

'They are burying Ocean?'
'They are.'

It was then I experienced one of those close connections between John Clare's world and my own. I had never seen Ocean, just as one rarely sees a legend, but I knew what she looked like, which is someone he would have seen—this in the purely native sense. Ocean was one of East Anglia's most celebrated Romanies. She had travelled our counties for nearly a century, leaving tales in her wake, a formidable woman with a magnificent name. And here she would lie, in our churchyard. There were family connections. Her grandsons, gone Gaujo, lived just up the road in a square bungalow at the edge of an

John Clare and the Gypsies

orchard which was never picked and behind windows which were never uncurtained. And there was a copse where she may have wintered.

Clare's gypsies were everywhere when I was a boy. They came regularly to the house, for mother would only have their split ash clothes pegs with the little tin band. And they did piece-work in summer, pea-picking, soft fruit gathering, hence the chalked board outside the pub, 'No Gypsies, no Travellers'. There was a green lane known as the Gull where we found stamped-out hearths and blackened cans, and evidence of ponies. In no time fireweed came to hide the mess. Grandmother, born the decade when Clare died, had actually witnessed a vardo being burnt on Lavenham common. Lavenham churchyard was full of Petulengros. George Borrow had put 'our' gypsies in *Romany Rye* and *Lavengro*. My old friend John Nash, wretched in the trenches, told me how he had been cared for by a young gypsy who had been called up and who comforted them both with promises of the Open Road. One day they would be 'out of all this' and on the Open Road. They would be friends and live again. On and on they would walk – in Buckinghamshire, which was where they truly belonged. No more Artists' Rifles, roll on sleeping in haystacks. John's only reading in Flanders was Borrow, and when Passchendaele threatened he sent *Lavengro* home to his girl for safety.

We knew a woman tramp called Nellie Eighteen and her lover Boxer who refused to sleep in the Spike (workhouse) and who resided briefly in ruined buildings of all kinds, and were accepted as part of the wandering population. Fanciful things were said about them. But they were tramps and not gypsies. We all knew the difference. You wouldn't find a gypsy pushing a pram.

Jonathan Bate wrote, 'Clare loved to spend time with the gypsies who camped on the commons and margins where they were to go once the "waste" grounds became private property. It was through such eyes as these that he saw enclosure.' The enclosure of Helpston put many of Clare's best-loved spots out of bounds, and not only sometimes out of bounds but beyond recognition, for they were in our terms bulldozed. His wrath flares up in poem after poem:

At Helpston

> The silver springs, grown naked dykes,
> Scarce own a bunch of rushes:
> When grain got high the tasteless tykes
> Grubbed up trees, banks and bushes,
> And me, they turned me inside out
> For sand and grit and stones
> And turned my old green hills about
> Picked my very bones.

He made Swordy Well protest. Bad enough for the villagers, now being pauperised, but quite terrible for the gypsies immemorially camped at Langley Bush. The Vagrancy Act of 1824, swiftly following the Enclosure Act, made it an offence, among other things, 'to be in the open air, or under a tent, or in a cart or wagon, not having any visible means of subsistence, and not giving a good account of himself, or herself'. Ocean had given a memorable account of herself, we believed. But for generations after the Vagrancy Act her kind were regularly sent to prison for merely existing. And then, only two years later, came the Commons Act of 1826 which allowed the local authority to set its own rules for its own common land. And soon most commons were closed to gypsies. When the Gypsy Council was at long last created in 1966, Gordon Boswell, a member of a leading gypsy family, at once proposed that permanent camps should be made by law where his people could winter without being moved on by the police. The Council was legally aided by Gratton Puxon, the son of a Colchester solicitor, who was a friend of ours. Gratton was the kind of practical romantic one would have met with among Clare's rural 'intellectuals', who thought and acted outside their own sphere, as it were.

Erotic gypsy women, with their freedom, were a frequent subject of Clare's songs during the asylum years.

> A gipsey lass my love was born
> Among the heaths furse bushes O,
> More fair than Ladies on the lawn,
> Whose song is like the thrushes O.
> Like links of snakes her inky hair,

> The dandy bean she kisses O.*
> Her face round as an apple fair
> She blisters where she kisses O.

(*There was an ancient law forbidding men to make love in a beanfield because its scent made them irresistible. Fellatio.)

And then we have 'Sweet legged' Sophie, and Maria 'who sleeps in the nightly dew'. He:

> Loves the flowers that she sees,
> The wild thyme bank she beds on
> Mid the songs of honey bees.

These 'cozy blanket camp' girls exist in a sexual dimension beyond the conventions. Free as air, the poet can take them at will. Part of Clare's life might be called a vagabondage in a native place. This is still not unusual for the artist/writer. He belonged as few writers have ever belonged – yet he knew that he did not belong. Not as the rest of his community belonged. His was the fate of the insider being an outsider. In order to write and read and look and listen, he would walk to the edge of his own birthright territory, and it was there that he would sometimes find those who quite clearly had no claim to it, the gypsies. He would spread himself on the earth where they had been.

Wednesday 29th Sept, 1824
> Took a walk in the fields ... saw an old woodstile taken away from
> a favourite spot which it had occupied all my life. The posts were
> overgrown with ivy and it seemed so akin to nature and the spot
> where it stood, as though it had taken it on lease for an undisturbed
> existence. It hurt me to see it was gone, for my affections claim a
> friendship with such things. Last year Langley Bush was destroyed,
> An old white thorn that had stood for more than a century full of
> fame. The Gipsies and Herd men all had their tales of its history.

A few weeks later Clare attended 'Another Gipsy Wedding of the

At Helpston

Smiths family, fiddling and drinking as usual'. He learned some gypsy medicine which was based on like for like, such as how to cure a viper's sting. Boil the viper and apply the broth to the wound it made. A sure cure, the gypsies said. Some of Clare's poems show both pride and prejudice for his Romany friends, calling them 'a sooty crew'. Though before this he assures them:

> That thou art reverenced, even the rude clan
> Of lawless Gipsies, driven from stage to stage,
> Pilfering the hedges of the husbandman ...

His frequent preferences for the parish boundary caused comment: 'My old habits did not escape notice – they fancied I kept aloof from company for some sort of study – others believed me crazed, and put some more criminal interpretation to my rambles and said I was a night-walking associate with the gipsies, robbing woods of the hares and pheasants because I was often in their company.' But sometimes he was at the camp for music lessons. A gypsy named John Gray was to teach him how to play the fiddle by ear: 'Finished planting my auricolas – went a-botanising after ferns and orchises, and caught a cold in the wet grass has made me as bad as ever. Got the tune of "Highland Mary" from Wisdom Smith, a gipsy, and pricked another sweet tune without a name as he fiddled it'. Jonathan Bate reminds us that Clare had been writing down dance tunes for many years, and that one of his oblong music books is entitled *A Collection of Songs, Airs and Dances for the Violin, 1818*. His fleeting vagabond Scottish grandfather had taught the villagers of Helpstone music among other subjects before going on his way. One of Clare's lime-burner workmates at Pickworth had actually joined the gypsies – married one of them. His name was James Nobbs. And such was their fascination that a Suffolk Archdeacon, Robert Hindes Groom, a friend of Edward FitzGerald and George Borrow, had also wed a Romany woman. A certain fastidiousness in Clare seems to have marked their relationship, their 'disgusting food' for instance. But he recognised their artistry, and he was an early precursor of folksong collecting. Recalling the 'No Peapickers' sign outside our Suffolk pubs when I was a boy reminds me of Vaughan Williams taking a young gypsy into a bar in order to take down his song – and both of them being thrown out by the landlord. It wasn't a 'singing' pub.

It was George Borrow, a near contemporary of John Clare, whose Romany books would offer an alternative life style to many Victorians. *Lavengro* was published In 1831, *The Romany Rye or the Gypsy Gentleman*, in 1857. Clare might well have read them at Northampton. Borrow was famously touchy and bad-tempered, and hard to handle. Stories of his picaresque wanderings and encounters are told in Spain, East Anglia and Wales to this day. During a walking holiday on Anglesey a few years ago my host said, 'George Borrow stayed in this house'. Returning from gathering material for *Hidden Wales* he saw a lad mending the roof and spoke to him in Welsh – and was answered in French. Much put out Borrow demanded to know why. 'Sir, you spoke to me in a language which is not your own, and I reply in a language which is not my own.' Speaking Romany became quite a cult in the nineteenth century although nothing like the heady cult of the Open Road. The Open Road cult descended from a celebrated passage in *Lavengro* which, if it had come John Clare's way during his last years in 'Hell', his other name for the 'Madhouse', would have sent shivers through him.

> 'Life is sweet, brother.'
> 'Do you think so?'
> Think so! There's night and day, brother, both sweet things; sun, moon, and stars, brother, all sweet things; there's likewise a wind on the heath. Life is very sweet, brother; who would wish to die?'
> 'I would wish to die – '
> 'You talk like a Gorgio – which is the same as talking like a fool. Were you a Romany Chal you would talk wiser. Wish to die, indeed! A Romany Chal would wish to live for ever.'
> 'In sickness, Jasper?'
> 'There's the sun and the stars, brother.'
> 'In blindness, Jasper?'
> 'There's the wind on the heath; if I could only feel that I would gladly live for ever.'

At Helpston

Two years after *Lavengro* was published, and still several years before death made it possible for Clare to return to Helpston, Matthew Arnold wrote *The Scholar-Gipsy*. It told of an Oxford undergraduate who walks out of the University, having seen through its claims, to join gypsy freedom. His life is furtive, shy like that of a woodland creature, and the world to which he belonged now has only glimpses of him. He is not pursued. His realm is Oxfordshire not Oxford, and the county is given a tempting pastorality which excludes such realities as the local vagabond law. Rather, the area is proud to harbour such a learned tramp. In his note on the poem Arnold said, 'After he had been pretty well exercised in the trade (of Romany lore), there chanced to ride by a couple of scholars, who had formerly been of his acquaintance. They quickly spied out their old friend among the gypsies; and he gave them an account of the necessity which drove him to that kind of life, and told them that the people he went with were not such impostors as they were taken for, but that they had a traditional kind of learning among them, and could do wonders by the power of the imagination, their fancy binding that of others ...' Arnold said too that he had found the story in Glanvil's *Vanity of Dogmatizing* (1661). *The Scholar-Gipsy* concludes with the wonderfully hazardous lines on how such a persistent foreign element may have reached our shore:

> Outside the western straits, and unbent sails
>   There, where down cloudy cliffs, through sheets of foam,
>   Shy traffickers, the dark Iberians come;
> And on the beach undid his corded bales.

During the High Beach exile, each winter surrounded by gypsy camps, Helpston dragged at Clare's thoughts all day long. Homesickness frequently overwhelmed him. The plants and birds of Epping Forest, the close-knit gypsy families with their music and nasty food and skinny dogs seemed like an extension of Helpston and yet was a hundred miles from it. One Sunday afternoon he met some gypsies who said he could hide away with them until there was a propitious moment for his escape from the madhouse. Money was mentioned. But Clare the patient did not have the same welcome as Clare the fiddler,

John Clare and the Gypsies

and the gypsies cleared off without helping him. When he went to their camp it was empty save for an old hat. He picked this up and kept it—may have worn it during the walk out of Essex. On Tuesday 20 July 1841, he took their suggested route. Epping was a very confusing place. When he at last managed to find the main road a man from the discouragingly named pub The Labour in Vain directed him towards Enfield – towards where Cowden Clarke had introduced Keats to Chaucer – and thus to the Great York Road. Now, as Clare wrote, it could only be 'plain sailing and steering ahead, meeting no enemy and fearing none'. 'Here shall he see no enemy but winter and rough weather.' Later he would give his own sanitized version of the gypsies. No pilfering, no stinking mutton, no being let down now. Just one more freedom song from a poor prisoner doing life:

> The joys of the camp are not cares of the Crown,
> There'll be fiddling and dancing a mile out of town.
> Will you come to the camp ere the moon goes down
>   A mile from the town?
>
> The camp of the gipsies is sweet by moonlight
> In the furze and the hawthorn – and all out of sight
> There'll be fiddling and dancing and singing tonight
>   In the pale moon light.

Orange-tip butterfly about to land

THOMAS HARDY AND JOHN CLARE

The opening lecture for the 11th International Thomas Hardy Conference at Dorchester, July 1994

In the nineteenth century two great English poets spoke for the farm labourers' 'condition' in a language which disturbed their readers. John Clare actually spoke directly from it. Thomas Hardy daringly elevated its so-called simple dramas to what he called 'Sophoclean' heights. John Clare, like Robert Burns, had touched the degrading soil. Thomas Hardy, although closely related to those who ploughed and sowed, had not.

   Recent biographers and literary critics have had to face up to both Clare's and Hardy's 'peasant' dilemma in order to make sense of both their genius and their predicament. Robert Gittings reminds us of the large number of labouring folk who were Hardy's relations, and whom he passed by. But I have frequently seen such apparently either snobbish or uncaring attitudes during funerals in our village church. One of the 'old people' dies and, behold, the church is, for half an hour, filled with the indigenous population, many of whom I learn only now belong to the dead person's family. 'Oh, yes, didn't you know, I am his cousin. She is my wife's aunt. That is his nephew, the one who went away ...'. And I have to tell myself that I have witnessed little or no acknowledgement of such relationships during the lifetime of the deceased. Weddings and funerals apart, closely related village people often have a way of living apart although they share the same few miles. In Clare's and Hardy's day, families were vast and full of secrets regarding blood relationships. They were also rather 'cool' – which was due, maybe, to the unmanageability of sustaining true family feeling on such a scale. And there was, too, that other reason, which I shall come to, for why John Clare and Thomas Hardy behaved as they did towards their roots – that local earth out of which sprang their greatness. To be any kind of writer where one was so deeply rooted could be an awkward business—still can. To be one who needed as much environmental nourishment as the crops themselves could be both a godsend and a disaster. John Clare and Thomas Hardy had everything they required for their inspiration to hand, and they knew it. Yet to translate such common stuff into the finest rural poetry and the finest rural novels in the language carried with it a personal exposure which was hard to bear. As we know to this very day, there is a fugitive aspect to every village. The indigenous writer or artist of any kind blows his own and his neighbours' cover, often injuring both himself and his background in the process. No one will ever know where Hardy and Clare 'got it from'. They are sports: odd, strange individuals who are at one and the same time 'one of us' – and yet clearly not one of us. They see what we refuse to see, or cannot see until it is pointed out to us. They are both reporters or chroniclers, and visionaries.

The conventional nineteenth-century reader was puzzled by what was then called 'peasant poetry'; they allowed for its novelty but nothing more. John Clare's publishers – who had published John Keats – promoted Clare as a second Robert Bloomfield. Bloomfield's long poem *The Farmer's Boy* appeared when Clare was a child – a real farmer's boy, a gardener's boy, pot-boy, a little working lad. It sold twenty-six thousand copies. And Clare himself was always to feel a tender affinity with the Suffolk poet whose origins, single burst of literary success and long years of subsequent neglect pitifully reflected his own background and experience. At the same time Clare, the next generation after Bloomfield, was not like him in any way except in his peasantry. He was more learned, more a naturalist, more a poet and, sadly, more grandly tragic. Robert Bloomfield did not work the soil but was exiled from it. In his famous poem he was a London shoemaker remembering his distant village, and who had become literate by reading the London newspapers. Because of his living in London, his ability to write poetry was less amazing than John Clare's ability to write his. There were no crushing village eyes to dodge. All the same, it was more Bloomfield's novelty value than being a writer in the usual sense which made his work sell. The literary establishment abused Keats for his 'cockney' nerve at daring to invade a classic territory, but

At Helpston

it gave Bloomfield a condescending pat on the head. And it did much the same twenty years later when Clare's startling collection *Poems Descriptive of Rural Life and Scenery* appeared in 1820 under the publishers' description of him as 'a Northamptonshire Peasant' – the kind of description which initially crippled Robert Burns.

John Clare was twenty-seven when he met his first and only fame. Not for the next century and a half would his rightful standing as the most direct voice of rural England be acknowledged. 'Where did he get it from?' was the question most asked in his own time. They knew where Mr Wordsworth and Mr Coleridge and Lord Byron got it from – and almost where poor young Keats got it from (not the best source) – but where did this little ploughman get it from? Clare's readers were both genuinely and sensationally interested. His reply to a question which dogged him all his life was, 'I kicked it out of the clods.' The poetry, he meant. The rudeness of the questioning received a rough answer which was no answer at all. It reminds us of Christ's first sermon in his local church, given when he was thirty – late in those days for such a debut. He had unrolled Isaiah and spoken so eloquently that those who had known him all his life were bewildered. 'Where does he get it from? Isn't he the carpenter's son?' They meant that he was not a graduate of the rabbinical schools and that neither until this moment had he shown any gift for language.

Both John Clare and Thomas Hardy were recognised by their mothers as being 'different' or special – or indeed odd. As we know, Hardy's mother (aided by his paternal grandmother) nourished the difference with her stream of dreadful tales about Napoleonic War soldiers, ferocious assize justice, rural melodramas, gossip and scandal. Mrs Clare could neither read nor write and, in her son's words, thought 'that the higher part of learning were the blackest arts of witchcraft'. Inadvertently she fed him with those insecurities which were to haunt the cottages right up to the Second World War. He added, however, that his mother's ambition 'ran high of being able to make me a good scholar as she had experienced enough in her own case to avoid bringing up her children in ignorance'. To make him literate, no more. But not to make him a poet – steer him clear of that, please God. Hardy's mother, on the other hand, was determined to give her son as excellent an education as possible and she offended those who charitably provided what they thought was sufficient learning for such a boy. Mrs Clare – 'God help her', wrote her son—had her 'hopeful and tender kindness crossed with difficulty, for there was often enough to do to "keep cart upon wheels", as the saying is, without incurring an extra expense of pulling me to school, though she never lost the opportunity when she was able to send me ? A penny a week could not always be found. But child-labour could. Jemima Hand, his grandmother would have none of this. Hardy seems never to have done anything manual, not even a bit of gardening. John Clare carried sacks of flour from the mill, toiled at The Blue Bell, the pub next to his parents' cottage, gardened for Lord Exeter, planted the quickset hedges around the village after it had been enclosed, and ploughed.

What the two poets did have in common was a physical slightness which could have been due to their difficult births. Clare was the weakest baby of twins – his sister died – and Hardy was thrown into a basket as stillborn until the midwife noticed that there was life in him. Clare was a small handsome man of five foot two – the same height as Keats. Hardy was taller and with the disproportionate head and body which one often sees in Victorian photographs. Both writers possessed a kind of watchfulness of expression which made them unusual, even beautiful at times. Both adored women. Each suffered and yet was made great because he could only 'breathe' his native air. This air was both vital – and tainted.

Although it is fanciful to dwell on possible meetings between writers, in Clare's case he would never have heard of Thomas Hardy, who was twenty-four when Clare died and had published nothing. The poor, everlastingly scribbling old man in the Northampton Asylum would not have known of Hardy's existence. Many years before, when Clare was in the Epping Asylum, young Alfred Tennyson was living next door and they might well have glimpsed each other, Clare toiling in the rascally Dr Allen's garden and Tennyson writing *In Memoriam*. Each would have heard the bells of 'Ring out, wild bells!' for they were those of Waltham Abbey. So, Tennyson in mourning, and Clare digging. Being a peasant, it was the policy of nearly all those who tried to help John Clare to set him to manual work.

At Helpston

But it came in handy. Throughout the splendid *The Shepherd's Calendar* we can see the literary strengths of Clare's agricultural skills and expertise. The hand which wrote 'The Nightingales Nest' stacked the sheaves. If Hardy knew of Clare's poems he never mentioned them. His 'Clare' was, of course, William Barnes. Barnes and Clare once wrote with a marvellously similar emotional quality on the same theme – the being forced to leave the old home. Barnes's poem is the unforgettable 'Woak Hill' of which E. M. Forster once said that 'if one has not tears in one's eyes at the end of "Woak Hill", one has not read it'. John Clare's poem on this subject is 'The Flitting', written after a kind but uncomprehending patron set the poet up in a cottage in a village which was not his own village:

> Strange scenes mere shadows are to me
> Vague unpersonifying things
> I love with my old haunts to be
> By quiet woods and gravel springs
> Where little pebbles wear as smooth
> As hermits beads by gentle floods
> Whose noises doth my spirits sooth
> And warms them into singing moods
>
> Here every tree is strange to me
> All foreign things where ere I go
> Theres none where boyhood made a swee
> Or clambered up to rob a crow
> No hollow tree or woodland bower
> Well known when joy was beating high
> Where beauty ran to shun a shower
> And love took pains to keep her dry...

William Barnes is still accused of inaccessibility because of his use of dialect, which astonished me, as it did E. M. Forster and countless other readers who knew nothing of Dorset's local language. Barnes was born eight years after Clare and outlived him by almost a quarter of a century. In the social terms of their day, Barnes the farmer's son, the schoolmaster and clergyman, would have belonged to a realm that was quite dizzily aloft from that the country-folk which he wrote about. And yet he articulates their very souls.

Clare's poetry is the English field given voice. There was no kicking it out of the clods but a profound drawing of it from both the cultivated and uncultivated land of his birthplace. If our farms and wildernesses could utter it would be in his words. His is a uniquely informed utterance. A huge reading as well as a constant contemplation of his native scenery, between them, produced in him a kind of rural scholarship which causes the modern student to alter his or her perception of what it was like to be a farm labourer in late-Georgian Britain. Simply because a shepherd or ploughman could not, or did not, write, we have no reason to believe that he did not feel or see the things which a realistic poet such as John Clare felt and saw. Or indeed, did not share William Barnes's knowledge of the innermost tenderness of humanity. John Clare's gradual collapse of health (exacerbated, as is so often the case, by 'helping hands' and pressures of all kinds) robbed us of what surely would have been one of the most remarkable rural works of all time, a 'peasant' naturalist's version of Gilbert White's classic *The Natural History of Selborne*. Fractions of this wonderful book appear in Margaret Grainger's *The Natural History Prose Writings of John Clare*.

The land and its workers also speak through Thomas Hardy with an authentic but different voice. It is the voice of the trapped, of men and women who are hedged in as much by what we now call the environment as by their parish boundaries. Not by any other writer is an indigenous group so fatally blown about by localised storms. *Far from the Madding Crowd*, published in 1874 when Hardy was 34, heralded his arrival as a great novelist. In this tale he spreads a few fields and pastures, a few houses, a few short travels in that humdrum direction or this, and a few villagers in stances which have been ordained by local tradition or by classical myths. So far, so familiar. But then Hardy does something not seen before. He gives his characters a double dimension, the one which they recognise and the one by which a Greek playwright would have recognised them. They work incessantly, and time for such business as making love or

At Helpston

sightseeing or gossiping has to be snatched. Talk takes place during tasks and if you wanted to do something extraordinary in the improving line, you hoped for a little accident or a brief illness. I once read of a nineteenth-century parson who, walking by a cottage about 9.30 p.m., heard a family singing Wesley's hymns and reproached it for not getting enough sleep to do its fieldwork efficiently. It was not uncommon for labourers to be given very small gardens so that all their energies went into their master's farm. ''Twas a bad leg allowed me to read the Pilgrim's Progress', says Joseph Poorgrass. Cain Ball managed a visit to Bath due to a respite from toil caused by having 'a felon upon his finger'. The plot of *Far from the Madding Crowd* is so firmly tied in to the implacable demands of work that an element of its comedy insists that, by right, there should be neither the strength nor the opportunity to do anything else. In Hardy leisure frequently breeds disaster. In *Far from the Madding Crowd*, and like John Clare, he saturates all the common knowledge of his home place with his reading. Hardy's intention, brilliantly realised, was a stylised actuality, the style being that of the classic pastoral, the actuality that of standard farming practice during the time of his mother's youth. He said that he meant to complete this novel 'within a walk of the district in which the incidents are supposed to occur', and that he found it 'a great advantage to be actually among the people described at the time of describing them'.

An advantage, yes, a comfort, no. They were too close for that. A few years later Hardy was to explain what he believed was the purpose of fiction. It was, he said, 'To give pleasure by gratifying the love of the uncommon in human experience, mental or corporeal', this succeeding most when the reader was made to feel that the characters were 'true and real like himself'. The critics were upset. How could farm-labourers ('peasant' was going out by the 1870s) think and hope and behave, well, like us? Whilst admitting that Mr Hardy had 'hit upon a new vein of rich metal for his fictitious scenes', a contemporary critic viewed Hardy's treatment of farm labourers with some irony: 'Ordinary men's notions of the farm labourer of the Southern counties have all been blurred and confused. It has been the habit of an ignorant and unwisely philanthropic age to look upon him as an untaught, unreflecting, badly paid, and badly fed animal, ground down by hard and avaricious farmers, and very little, if at all, raised by intelligence above the brutes and beasts to whom he ministers.'

Such remarks in a review of *Far from the Madding Crowd*, in the *Saturday Review*, shockingly illuminate the predicament of John Clare half a century earlier. In 1823 he was at the pinnacle of his brief celebrity. Here was a peasant writing books! Here was a peasant who had been to London and who had hobnobbed with men of letters, Coleridge, Lamb, Hazlitt. Taylor the publisher, still with the once bestselling Robert Bloomfield in mind, exulted in this phenomenon and he worked hard to polish up Clare's grammar in order that ladies and gentlemen would be able to read his work. In vain the poet protested. The miracle – or novelty – was that he could write verse. It need only be made readable. His publisher promoted Clare but wrecked his poetry, and there was little he could do about it. He was a peasant and had to be guided. The restoration of Clare's text during the 1960s onwards (plus our ever-increasing interest in the countryside) has uncovered a Clare as fresh and captivating as a landscape from which the varnish and dirt of ages have been skilfully removed.

Far from the Madding Crowd is set between two long stretches of agricultural depression and in what historians like to dub 'a golden age'. In his later novels, Hardy would be accused of darkening the English countryside for his own melodramatic purposes. The truth of the matter was that towards the close of the nineteenth century, and a whole hundred years after the birth of John Clare, the lives of Britain's farmworkers had become so poverty-stricken and tragic that the Norfolk novelist Mary Mann, herself a farmer's wife, could look at their lot and presume that only some grim purpose known to God could justify it. In Hardy's essay 'The Dorsetshire Labourer', written in 1883, we have a direct piece of rural sociology which reveals how much he knew of what was going on all around him. And yet he could say, quite truthfully in certain respects, 'that happiness will find her last refuge on earth [among those who till the soil], since it is among them that a perfect insight into the conditions of existence will be longest postponed'. Where ignorance is bliss, in other words.

At Helpston

Impertinent questions drew Clare's response that he kicked his poems out of the clods. Does Thomas Hardy celebrate the life of the (human) clod? Never. This slur on village England he refutes from the very beginning. For one thing, it was too near home. Yet the problem of animating what had, until he began to write, been ignored as being below the level of polite interest, or as being simply lumpen, would have been insuperable had he tried to work it out. But he did not. What he did was to write so superbly about his own people that it made it pointless to ask, 'Why these poor toilers?' Behind him lay the harsh facts of Jemima's youth. All around him lay a mass of inherited material of every kind: the best, the worst. In a poem called 'Spectres that Grieve', one of many which are threnodies for the ordinary country folk, Hardy makes the dead who have been denied a proper history by their so-called betters, protest from the grave:

> We are stript of rights; our shames lie unredressed,
> Our deeds in full anatomy are not shown,
> Our words in morsels merely are expressed
> On the scriptured page, our motives blurred, unknown.

Much of Hardy's work defends the dispossessed. But it has to do so from a height. Being what he was, he could not be what he had come from. Similarly John Clare. This is the dilemma of the great writer or artist who stays at home. Hardy's actual touching-the-soil poems are few and far between. One is 'The Farm-Woman's Winter':

> I
> If seasons all were summers,
>   And leaves would never fall,
> And hopping casement-comers
>   Were foodless not at all,
> And fragile folk might be here
>   That white winds bid depart;
> Then one I used to see here
>   Would warm my wasted heart!

II
One frail, who, bravely tilling
    Long hours in gripping gusts,
Was mastered by their chilling,
    And now his ploughshare rusts.
So savage winter catches
    The breath of limber things,
And what I love he snatches,
    And what I love not, brings.

Hardy is unusual as a writer in that he lets characters from his novels have an extra life in his poems. There is 'Tess's Lament', and in 'The Pine Planters' we have Marty South, the heroine of *The Woodlanders*, having to fell trees alongside the lover who refuses to look at her. Their actions are mechanical:

We work here together
    In blast and breeze;
He fills the earth in,
    I hold the trees.

He does not notice
    That what I do
Keeps me from moving
    And chills me through.

He has seen one fairer
    I feel by his eye,
Which skims me as though
    I were not by.

And since she passed here
    He scarce has known
But that the woodland
    Holds him alone.

At Helpston

> I have worked here with him
>   Since morning shine,
> He busy with his thoughts
>   And I with mine...

But it was for Hardy the desolate fields of Flintcomb-Ash which represented the nadir of farm toil. It is where poor Tess ends up when she is reduced, as so many women were, to near-slavery. In 'We Field-Women' Hardy shows this place in varying degrees of weather:

>   How it rained
> When we worked at Flintcomb-Ash,
> And could not stand upon the hill
> Trimming swedes for the slicing-mill.
> The wet washed through us – plash, plash, plash:
>   How it rained!
>
>   How it snowed
> When we crossed from Flintcomb-Ash
> To the Great Barn for drawing reed,
> Since we could nowise chop a swede.
> Flakes in each doorway and casement-sash:
>   How it snowed!
>
>   How it shone
> When we went from Flintcomb-Ash
> To start at dairywork once more
> In the laughing meads, with cows three-score,
> And pails, and songs, and love – too rash:
>   How it shone!

But of course it is in his magnificent set pieces of the farming year, such as the famous scene in chapter 22 of *Far from the Madding Crowd* in which shearing is given a sumptuous treatment unlike anything previously seen in literature, that Thomas Hardy reveals the closeness of his eye, if not his hand, to his local earth. Similarly, the description of the patriarchal splendours about dairying in Tess where a Dorset farmer controls a world like that of Abraham. In such scenes Hardy challenges every previous concept of the 'simple task' and directs the reader's vision to a view of labour which holds within it those satisfactions which are usually found in poetry and religion. His story-telling is filled with meditation. One is made aware of his divided intelligence as he sees life as the shearers see it, and then as he himself sees it. Joseph Poorgrass sums up the whole business of farming with his, ''Tis the gospel of the body, without which we perish, so to speak it.'

John Clare would have agreed. But his position was a complex one. When a man ploughs, it is with one foot in the furrow and one on the level. It makes a rough progress, up and down, up and down. He was the peasant; he was the supreme English poet of the countryman's experience. Eventually – one could say inevitably – the unevenness tripped him into Northampton General Lunatic Asylum where, far from insane most of the time, he wrote. With little else to do, the output was enormous – and uneven. This cache of sometimes earthbound, often soaring rural poetry lay mostly buried until the 1920s onwards, when writers such as Edmund Blunden, the Tibbles, Geoffrey Grigson, Geoffrey Summerfield and Eric Robinson brought it into the sunlight.

The progress of agriculture is a kind of Alps, all peaks and plunges. For so natural an activity, it is strangely precarious and easily ruinous. Clare and Hardy sang its heights and charted its depths. Clare lived through the trauma of Enclosure, cursing its evils, and then through the bitter years of Chartism. Hardy was just at the beginning of his career when a biblical spell of rain washed away all the brief farming prosperity of the 1850s and brought in the long years of depression. By the 1890s, when he renounced novel-writing for poetry, there began what they called 'the flight from the land' as the labourers fled from agricultural misery. At this moment another young writer, Henry Rider Haggard, who had made a name with exciting adventure stories about Africa and who in his thirties was now farming in Norfolk, tried to halt the exodus. All this just a century after the birth of Clare and just when Hardy had abandoned fiction.

Clare was in continuous flight from the land as workplace, but only

At Helpston

to find his true working place in the little hidden copses and dells and woods where he could write unseen and undisturbed and especially unnoticed. His and Hardy's poetry differed because one touched and the other watched the soil. Each fully understood its majesty and its treachery. Clare's work is alternately a *Te Deum* and a *De Profundis* to the cultivated and uncultivated acres of his native Helpston, the place of endless work and endless dreams.

A cow crossing the dyke, 1991

JOHN CLARE IN SCOTLAND

A number of recent experiences and readings came together to suggest the subject of this chapter. First, I had just come back from Scotland, staying with friends at Kinloch Rannoch. This was in fact a retreat, a party of eight including two botanists, in a big white lonely house above Loch Rannoch, and backing onto Rannoch Moor, one of Britain's mighty desolations. One of these annual walks isn't more than two miles from a deserted stone village which belonged to the notorious Highland Clearances, when landowners like the Duchess of Sutherland preferred sheep to men. There it lay, a biggish place with crofts and barns and tracks, and drovers' roads, by a flashing burn, with sheep in residence, and the strong pattern of long habitation by men, women and children, ancestors now of prosperous folk in Canada and New Zealand.

And then, my neighbour Mr Brown died, aged a hundred; born at Michaelmas, died at Michaelmas. When he was three his father had hired a train which brought this Ayrshire family from the tough Lowlands to the South-east of England, and he as a little boy heard, and remembered, the kicking of the plough horses in their box as the special train, hired for ten pounds, brought everything the Browns possessed, their farm gear, their stock, their chattels, their corn seed, to East Anglia. He only once returned to Scotland, and this was in his seventies, when he took his grandson to see the obelisk commemorating their ancestor on the moor, the young crofter shot by Claverhouse's men for being a Covenanter. And one of his constant requests, when he came to talk to me once a week, was to look up certain Scottish words in the glossary at the back of my copy of Burns's Poems, for they were, in his nineties, slipping away from him. At his funeral the church, at which I had to give the Address, was filled with Norfolk, Suffolk and Essex Scottish farmers of the third generation of immigrants.

At Helpston

When I first walked in Scotland, during my twenties, my bible was Boswell's *Life of Johnson* with its great *Tour of the Hebrides*. And it is the notoriously unpromising first encounter of these two unlikely friends which brought John Clare's grandfather into some kind of focus. I'll remind you of what happened when Boswell met Johnson. The great man was fifty-four, the mighty biographer was twenty-three. Boswell was longing to meet Johnson when, whilst having tea with Mr Davies the bookseller in the back parlour of his shop, the door was darkened by a terrifying figure. Boswell went to pieces. 'Don't tell him where I come from', he begged Mr Davies. 'From Scotland!' said the wicked bookseller. 'Mr Johnson, I do indeed come from Scotland, but I cannot help it.' 'That, Sir, I find, is what a very great many of your countrymen cannot help,' was the reply. The year was 1763. Less than twenty years after the 'Forty-five, young Scots were on the road, and twenty years after this, Dr Johnson was still telling poor Boswell, 'Sir, the noblest prospect that a Scotchman ever sees is the high road that leads him to London'.

The effects of all diaspora, artistically as well as socially, are incalculable. Clare is constantly thought of as the epitome of the local village voice which articulates what is said and done and thought in one little place for centuries. And yet at the very moment when James Boswell came to London, Clare's grandfather came to Helpston from Scotland, not a ploughman like Burns, looking for a way out of rural poverty, but an itinerant schoolmaster. How and why he entered Helpston we may never discover. Maybe it was because there were possible patrons all around: Lord Exeter, Earl Fitzwilliam, the Trollope family at Torpel, even Christ's College, Cambridge. Or it may be simply because the Great North Road passed by this village, and the Scots perhaps sheltered in it on their long walk to London. This wanderer's name, as we know, was John Donald Parker. He could play the violin, and he was educated. If they would find him somewhere to live, and would feed him, he would teach their children to read and write, as well as play the violin at the dances. John Donald's special friend was Lord Manners's head gardener, and his love was Alice Clare, the Parish Clerk's daughter. When she became pregnant he vanished. But, genetically, the harm or the good had been done. And such blood mixes have been achieved ever since some Irish playboy walked the Icknield Way. Alice called her boy Parker; Parker's son called him 'one of fate's chancelings who drop into this world without the honour of matrimony'. As John Clare's grandmother lived to be eighty-three, making him twenty-seven when she died, there can be no doubt that he would have heard a good deal about his Scottish grandfather. John Clare and his twin sister were themselves conceived out of wedlock. The Parish Registers of England unblushingly tell us how this was the rule rather than the exception.

By the time Clare reached what might be called his Scottish Period among the books at Northampton Asylum his quarter-native land was no longer derided by England because of the Rebellion and its uncouthness, but had become the most Romantic country in the whole of Europe because of Sir Walter Scott's Waverley Novels, and Queen Victoria's preference for it above any place else in the world. And as for Robert Burns, it was his poetry, along with the Bible, that accompanied the great exodus to the four corners of the British Empire, and which held the Scots culturally together. Wherever they happened to settle, they would have known these two books, and it wouldn't be entirely far-fetched to imagine that John Clare, exiled from his beloved Helpston for almost three decades, began at Northampton to relate to another place which was partly genuinely his, and to use its language with far greater claim to it than many who now sported the once-banned tartans.

And thus the Scottish poems need not be seen as pastiche, but legitimate, if sometimes Burns-imitative, to what genuinely belonged to Clare himself. Thomas Hardy learned more about life in the countryside from his grandmother than from his own mother, and John Clare, aged twenty-seven when his grandmother Alice died, could have been made to feel his Scottishness. He knew his *difference* from the beginning. It was a painful, uncomfortable, yet triumphant knowledge. The Scottishness of Clare hasn't of course been missed by Clare scholars. In a fascinating essay entitled 'John Clare: the trespasser', John Goodridge and Kelsey Thornton show the poet being drawn to both gypsies and to the Scottish drovers who, as brown-skinned and exotically attired as the gypsies, with their bits of plaid

At Helpston

and blankets and strange speech, created a sensation as they passed through Northamptonshire.* And they quote his description of them in the 'July' section of *The Shepherd's Calendar*:

>Along the roads in passing crowds
>Followd by dust like smoaking clouds
>Scotch droves of beast a little breed
>In swelterd weary mood proceed
>A patient race from scottish hills
>To fatten by our pasture rills
>Lean wi the wants of mountain soil
>But short and stout for travels toil
>Wi cockd up horns and curling crown
>And dewlap bosom hanging down
>Followd by slowly pacing swains
>Wild to our rushy flats and plains
>At whom the shepherds dog will rise
>And shake himself and in supprise
>Draw back and waffle in affright
>Barking the traveller out of sight
>And mowers oer their scythes will bear
>Upon their uncooth dress to stare
>And shepherds as they trample by
>Leaves oer their hooks a wondering eye
>To witness men so oddly clad
>In petticoats of banded plad
>Wi blankets oer their shoulders slung
>To camp at night the fields among
>When they for rest on commons stop
>And blue cap like a stocking top
>Cockt oer their faces summer brown
>Wi scarlet tazzeles on the crown
>Rude patterns of the thistle flower
>Untrickd and open to the shower
>And honest faces fresh and free
>That breath[e] of mountain liberty

The static, trapped, parochial nature of the farm-worker thrills to any passing invasion, and always has. Hardy saw the excitement when soldiers from the local barracks were sent to help with the harvest, which he called 'a little red among the corn' and which created great emotions among the girls. And in my lifetime pea-picking itinerants and tramps and Irish travellers all, as Clare said, caught the eye, and captured the imagination. But the Scottish drovers did more than this. They spoke of relationship to him, of mutuality, of something shared. Theirs wasn't the outcast freedom of gypsies, but freedom within the rural structure itself. And the Scottish connection was freely claimed at Northampton. Among Clare's books was the 1817 edition of Burns's poetical works, as well as the five volume 1814 edition which included the letters added by Sir Walter Scott. Also, *Poems & Songs Chiefly in the Scottish Dialect* by Robert Tannahill, the young Paisley weaver. But as Goodridge and Thornton state in their essay, the young Clare was as overwhelmed as the rest of the world by the Waverley Novels themselves, and phrases such as 'Heart of Midlothian' and 'Sweet Lammermore' appear in his poems, as well as a distinctly un-Romantic rebelliousness which came from his knowledge of the Scottish struggle after the 'Forty-five.

He began writing Scottish poems at High Beech, Epping, one of the earliest being:

> Heres a health unto thee bonny lassie O
> Leave the thorns o' care wi' me
> And whatever I may be
> Here's happiness to thee
> Bonny lassie O

a variation on Thomas Lyle's 'Let us haste to Kelvingrove'. From then on, until the end of his life, Scotland and Northamptonshire ran together, as do certain estates, with often no clearly marked border between them. A great many of these Scottish Northamptonshire poems are an amorous balladry, about Sally and Susan, and Alice and Ann and Phoebe and Mary, and lassies generally, whose wistful eroticism usually went no further than what would be permissible to

At Helpston

recite at a party. We are inclined to flinch politely at the Clare which they reveal, but like Burns he was a man who adored women, who was married, who had had loves and lovers of all kinds, but who, for nearly thirty years, was denied this kind of companionship. The Mary and the Bonny Ann poems, etc., are often exquisite. But some are conventional or banal. All witness to a hunger for women's company, to Clare the lover. Many were written in 1845. He was then in his early fifties, and the Scottish ballad discipline allowed him to call back, as it were, the girls of his boyhood. In August 1848 at the asylum they found a bit of paper in his pocket which read:

> Some pretty face, remembered in our youth
> Seems ever with us, whispering Love and Truth

Nor is it likely that a poet who kept meticulous inventories of all kinds, about nature, and rural tasks, and village people, wouldn't find some way of making a calendar of girls. For whilst these occupied a single place in his heart, geographically they were often in two places at once, Lolham Brigs and the Highlands. But what could be more legitimate for such heroines? He manages the Scottish dialect well, and although he possessed glossaries of it, there is a sense in his use of it that he had often heard it spoken, perhaps at Helpston. We know that occasionally he had a Scottish visitor, such as John Ramsay, the Kilmarnock poet, and knew the work of the Scottish songwriter Robert Tannahill, and his fine ear for language and lilt gave his Scottish writing a certain authenticity. He was by nature an escapee, a man who had to mount various barriers which would have confined him, one way or another, since his birth. And at Northampton, outlawed from the freedoms which he had created for himself at Helpston, he took claim to his Scottish inheritance. Sally Frisby, a Helpston girl, who died in 1819 aged 22, and Phoebe from the Rose and Crown at Oundle, whom he had met when he was a militiaman, and Mary King, also from Helpston, 'as brown as a boy', would be amazed to have found themselves translated to the mountains and the heather, but this is what he did for them. And sometimes, as in the beautiful 'White Thorn Tree', written at Northampton in 1845, he sent Helpston itself north.

John Clare in Scotland

The one girl who doesn't receive the Scottish treatment is Mary Joyce. She is always with Clare as she was back home at Glinton long ago:

> I sleep with thee and wake with thee
> And yet thou art not there
> I fill my arms with thoughts of thee
> And press the common air

Towards the end of his life comes a very interesting poem. A young Scotsman is trying to persuade his girlfriend to leave an English village. Might John Parker have been unsuccessful in persuading Alice to leave home? Perhaps he did not desert her. Perhaps she refused to accompany him north:

> 1
> Will ye gang wi' me to Scotland dear
> Where the mountains touch the sky
> And leave your humdrum labours here
> And climb the hills sa'e high
> Come leave your fowl your pigs and kye
> And your mud-floor dwelling here
> come put your wheel and knitting bye
> We'll be off to Scotland dear
> For the summer lark is in the sky
>
> 2
> The daisys gold in silver rim
> Is blazing on the mountain side
> And the skylarks wing in the sky grows dim
> While the clouds like racers ride
> So come with me to Scotland dear
> And thy tartan plaid put on
> The swallow has come to the new green year
> And we'll to Scotland now be gone
> So go wi' me to Scotland dear
> Ere the winter of lifes comes on

At Helpston

                3
And go with me to Scotland dear
And leave your English home
The gowans bloom, and the scented brere
Will tempt your steps to roam
And go with me to Scotland dear
Where the crimpled brackens grow
Where the rose blooms on the mountain brere
As white as driven snow
Then in the green bloom of the year
With me to Scotland go

As I said, he was now right in the Heart of Midlothian, and a far country to which he was by blood attached had become, under Walter Scott's banner, a marvellous freedom, and Clare himself a freeman of it. He wrote to Patty that the asylum was 'the purgatorial hell and French bastile of English liberty, where harmless people are trapped and tortured until they die'. Poem after poem after this has titles like 'To Liberty', 'The Thistle', 'Scotland', 'My Heart is in Scotland', and 'On the bleak hills of Scotland my fancy reposes'. They reveal Clare's knowledge of the years of defeat following Culloden, and the years of recovery partly due to a novelist, of the Scottish fate to be exiled but to come home at the last.

  Young husbands go to sea in the poems, they go to sea at Leith in order to make some money for their families. Women – and sometimes Clare puts himself in the Scottish wife's or girlfriend's position – they simply wait. One says:

    I like the lad that's like mysel
    Content to be alain
    Though he's not a penny for to tell
    And sits on the hearth stane
    If hes a man—a comely man
    My sweet heart he shall be
    Contentment is the choicest plan
    Love makes us baith agree ...

John Clare in Scotland

> I'll luiv and keep him all my sen
> And gie him a' my heart
> To me he'll be the man o' men
> Love's wholly not a part
> I hate to ain ye bit o' men
> Like Tailors cabbage gear
> Ill be his woman every night
> He my man a' the year

Well, contentment is not a virtue that Clare, inured at Northampton, would ever know. Just as at Helpston, he had all kinds of restless journeys to the lonely kingdoms of birds and flowers, and where gypsies and herdboys and shepherds and drovers sat around fires in the dark nights, mysterious and outside things, in a country which was beyond the parish limits.

And so at Northampton he set out on those piles of rough paper his grandfather's world of mountains and firs and burns and lassies. The injustice done to it joining the injustice being done to himself would not be comfortable, but it would be just. And he had got the climate of Scotland exactly:

> 1
>
> The rauk o' the hills & the mist o' the mountains
> Like the reek o' a pot and the smoke o' a kill
> Draws further off still while the round sun is counting
> His pulses o' light i' the morning sae still
> Saftly and chill comes the breeze o' the ocean
> Saft fans the brackin alang the hill side
> The vale o' green broom-twigs are a' easy motion
> Like a green sea o' waters wi' waves rolling wide
>
> 2
>
> O maid o' the mountain here's scenes that would please ye
> Would ye climb but as high at the break o' the day
> Walk wi' me o'er their taps love and make your life easy
> And look o'er the ocean mist mealy and grey

At Helpston

>Life and its cares will be under our feet love
>Like a hawk that is cheated or a foe led astray
>We can look on sweet nature in cold or in heat love
>Unseen on the mountain tops a' the lang day
>
>>3
>
>There's the clumps o' rest harrow luv' purple and yellow
>There's the bushes o' sweet-briar luscious and sweet
>There's the swallow that twitters and fallows his fellow
>Like birds o' the ither world under our feet
>Come to the mountain tops soon after day break
>Where toads canna' climb and birds seldom fly
>There's a place i' the rock where a biggin we make
>And true love will welcome they presence with joy

* * *

The last poem Clare wrote before his death in 1864 was called 'Birds Nests', and he prefaced it with two lines from Robert Burns's 'Tam O'Shanter', which is one of the poems I used to have to read to Mr Brown:

>That night, a child might understand
>The Deil had business on his hand

'Tam O' Shanter', you will recall, is about someone who is temporarily out of his wits, and who goes through hell and high water before being restored to sanity, to his farm, to his wife, by a guardian angel-*cum*-mare Maggie. Shanter was a farm on the Carrick coast and Tam who owned it a character well-known for getting drunk in Ayr on market day and being brought safely home by his faithful horse. John Clare knew all about haunted roads and terrors by the way, and about the warmth of the inn dissipating into cold horror on the dark road. As he says in his autobiography, as a boy running errands along the Maxey lane, he was so frightened by the local ghosts that he used to try and fill his mind with poetry in order to leave no room for them when he

John Clare in Scotland

passed their 'registered' spots. Burns carries the popular plight of the drunk farmer beyond a joke – carries him into a satanic world which Clare would have glimpsed when sick. His bogies were real enough.

* John Goodridge and Kelsey Thornton, 'John Clare: the Trespasser', in Hugh Haughton et al (eds), *John Clare in Context* (Cambridge: Cambridge University Press, 1994), 87-129.

A hedge in November, 1984

THE HELPSTON BOYS

Boyhood is a recurring theme with John Clare. His own and that of his contemporaries make lively passages in his work. The persistence of the theme is partly deliberate, partly unconscious. He was both recording and re-imagining his time, his geography, his ethos, himself, his companions, with the result that we find it impossible to recognise what he was finally to describe as 'this sad non-identity'. The first and last things which a writer must do is to know what and who he is. Clare had cause to struggle to remember both states. To know that one can never be what one was, as did Coleridge, can be devastating. Rimbaud, amazingly, knew as much at twenty and wrote no more.

John Clare was less a visionary than a remembrancer. All he saw ahead of him was what appeared on countless country tombstones, the word Rest, which was the labourer's description for his final 'escape'. Yet Clare knew that for him there could be neither rest nor escape even when he was an old man in the asylum because he had brought his youthful landscape with him and everyone with whom he had shared it. There he was by the bridge, the fourteen year-old lover. Whatever happened, it was soon put a stop to. Although 'thwarted', his love for Mary Joyce lasted all his life. It was to keep him boyish in this passionate respect, this love between two village children. Rather like Thomas Hardy after forty years of loveless marriage, the courtship which preceded it would grow more wonderful as time passed.

And then, as we know, the 1809 Act for Enclosing Lands in the Parishes of Maxey with Deepingate, Northborough, Glinton with Peakirk and Helpstone made 'all that map of boyhood overcast'. We tend to confine Clare in his own parish boundaries but forget that the first instinct of a village boy is to jump over them, so to speak, to go wild out of sight. Clare cursed Enclosure then leaped over it, to where

> Unbounded freedom ruled the wandering scene
> Nor fence of ownership crept in between
> To hide the prospect of the following eye
> Its only language was the circling sky
> One mighty flat undwarfed by bush & tree
> Spread its feint shadow of immensity
> And lost itself which seemed to eke its bounds ...
> Fence now meets fence in owners little bounds
> Of fields & meadows large as garden grounds
> In little gardens little minds to please
> With men & flocks imprisoned ill at ease
>   (*Poems of the Middle Period*, II, p. 347-9)

So 'all that map of boyhood was overcast' by the time Clare was eighteen. Yet during the long last decades of his existence at Northampton, when there would have been no shape or pattern to anything had he not created them, the first country of his love and poetry was given back its every feature. There is frank mourning, rather than nostalgia, but there is as well the happy outdoors of the Georgian village youth in all his toiling, idling, playing state. An account which is unequalled as an inventory because there is no deliberate attempt to list everything. The pros or cons are hard upon each other's heels. For the poet himself

> There are spots where I played, there are spots where I loved
> There are scenes where the tales of my choice were approved
> As green as at first—and their memory will be
> The dearest of lifes recollections to me—
> The objects seen there in the care of my heart
> Are as fair as at first—and will never depart
>   ('Stanzas', *Later Poems*, I, p. 395)

'Who owns the land?' asks the child who is working at ten years old.

> They told me God the land possessed
>   The bushes trees and flowers

At Helpston

> That every soul thereon was blest
>   And all its joy was ours
> That God they hummed their spirits joy
>   Was both the King and Prince
> I saw it when a little boy
>   But never found it since
>   ('Stanzas', *Later Poems*, I, p.575)

Not on the map of Northamptonshire. Like every county this was filled with noisy labouring children. Clare's *The Shepherd's Calendar* is loud with their singing and shouting, their whistling and general hubbub. A similar hullabaloo fills Parson Woodforde's *Diary* in which Norfolk boys with Shakespearian names, Brettingham Scurl and Barnabas Woodcock, help to keep the Rectory in an uproar. Clare notes 'the happy dirty driving boy', the 'bawling' herd boy, the merry cries of sliding boys and the fanciful shepherd boy. Shepherds were the proto-poets and seers. He sees the dinner boy, the bird-scaring boy and the boys at the shearing, all of them briefly and wonderfully wild until

> Reason like a winters day
> Nipt childhoods visions all away
> Those truths are fled and left behind
> A real world and a troubling mind

Clare, of course, as with all artists and writers, failed to have his childhood vision nipt away, hence his grown-up dilemma, hence his genius, hence his suffering and, at long-last recognised, hence his unique achievement. Holding on to his early vision for the rest of his life, he was able to make use of it until the end. Thus his constant refrain of 'When I was a boy' as he began on a very grown-up subject. Take the mindless tradition of the countryman's cruelty to animals, the casual killing of anything which swam, flew or ran by the village boy. The naturalist and the poet have always condemned this sport, but none as painfully as John Clare, and at a time when such slaughter was the chief recreation of the male teenager. Fed by the myths of gamekeepers, blooded by their fathers and employers, curiously excited by badger baiting and the little woodland Tyburns where moles, weasels and other creatures hung in rows as a lesson to every other animal, heartlessly amused by the behaviour of mother birds finding that their nests had been robbed, obscene with frogs, his Helpston boys did no more than every country lad in England did – and would go on doing until film brought the age of enlightenment. Clare balances this infantile killing with the adult killing by sportsmen, and puts both on a par with the new agriculture where 'the axe of the spoiler' destroyed all the tender associative things. 'All levelled like a desert by the never weary plough'. His condemnation strikes a modern note.

> Inclosure like a Buonaparte let not a thing remain
> It levelled every bush and tree and levelled every hill
> And hung the moles for traitors – though the brook is running still
> It runs a naked stream cold and chill
> (from 'Remembrances', *Poems of the Middle Period*, IV, p.130)

Searching for his own cover in order to read, he said, 'It is common in villages to pass judgment on a lover of books as a sure indication of laziness.' Four years earlier William Hazlitt, daring to read in a country inn, was driven out by the jeering labourers. Driven also to write one of his matchless pieces of invective on the special horribleness of rural intolerance. Clare was not alone in his search for concealment. Heaths and copses, pools and warrens, dens and the deep woods were where boys became men. He discovered that he could have a barn all to himself on a Sunday. His first letters were made in barn-dust. It reminds us of William Bewick the engraver who was allowed by the kind vicar to draw his first pictures on the flagstones in the church. Clare condemned the sole use of the Bible and Prayer Book as reading primers in the village school. To make them 'task books' was to put the children off reading altogether.

It is less in his brief *Sketches in the Life of John Clare by Himself* than in his natural history prose writings that we discover his true boyhood, as it were. For here more even than in *The Shepherd's Calendar* does it unconsciously appear. 'When I was a boy I used to be very curious to watch the nightingale'. The word 'watch' instead of

At Helpston

listen is revelatory. 'When I was a boy I kept a tame cock sparrow three years.' 'When I was a boy I was attacked by an owl'. 'When I was a boy there was a little spring of beautiful soft water which was never dry. It used to dribble its way through the grass in a little ripple of its own making, no bigger than a grip or cart-rut. And in this little springhead there would be hundreds of little fish called a minnow. We used to go on Sunday in harvest and deck [bail] it out with a dish and string the fish on rushes ... thinking ourselves great fishers ...' When old and shut away, such limpid boyhood observations would return to him and he would thread them into his poems. Some were threaded into 'Little Trotty Wagtail', written in the asylum when he was fifty-one, and the only poem of his which most people knew until the nineteen-thirties.

> – How happy seem
> Those schoolboy friendships leaning oer the style
> Both reading in one book ...
> Ah happy boys well may ye turn and smile
> When joys are yours that never cost a sigh
> (from 'Evening School Boys', Poems of the Middle Period, IV, p.149)

A young confident moorhen

SOLVITUR AMBULANDO: CLARE AND FOOTPATH WALKING

None of us now realise what walking was like to the people who lived in villages like Helpston, all over Britain, for centuries. In her interesting study *The English Path* (1979) Kim Taplin wonders why this, one of the main routes to our literature, particularly our poetry, has received so little social investigation. There are plenty of books on roads, but few explanations of paths. We do of course have a whole library on roads, rambling, and walking these days. But the study of paths themselves is as fugitive as these tracks, which have to be traced through our own rural world and rural writers alike, for us to have any real knowledge of them. One of Kim Taplin's chapters is called *Solvitur Ambulando*. She describes this as an 'old Latin tag [which] means something like "you can sort it out by walking"'. She continues:

> Working out, finding out, unknotting and freeing are all possible connotations of the word *solvitur*, and in this chapter I want to look at the claims of certain writers for the benefits of footpath walking to the spirit. Andrew Young used the words in his poem *A Traveller in Time*:
>
>> Where was I? What was I about to see?
>> *Solvitur ambulando*.
>> A path offered its company
>
> A companionable path was more apt for a curative release than a road, since solitude, peace, and close contact with nature, as well as the action of walking, are all important ingredients. Problems unravel as the feet cover the miles, but through the body's surroundings, as well as the body's action. (p. 103)

At Helpston

My own existence is as controlled by footpaths as those of my farming ancestors in Suffolk. Friends have often told me that my life would be transformed if I drove a car, forgetting how transformed it has been because I don't. And so I walk a mile of flinty track to fetch the milk, and two miles to the village post office, church or pub, and more miles too when I get stuck with my writing, and wander off to the river path for a little *solvitur ambulando*. So I have done since a boy, in these more or less same scenes. And so of course did most of our forbears, including quite recent ones. And did we but comprehend it, a great amount of our best poetry, novels and essays smell, not of the lamp, but of dust, mud, grit, pollen, and, I expect, sweat. Even the clergy took to the inspiring tramp via something called a 'sermon walk'. There was one at Little Easton rectory, where I used to stay a long time ago. It was a long lawn between discreet hedges and borders, where the Rector could stroll up and down, spinning thoughts around his text for Sunday.

John Clare is the genius of the footpath. So poignant is his statement on the road that it tends to overlay his many and various statements on the footpaths. That wretched road journey, in July 1841, just after his forty-sixth birthday, when he was alone, weakening and penniless, and when he had to, as he said, 'lay down with my head towards the north to show myself the steering point in the morning', was a walk entirely isolated from every other walk he had, or made, or would ever make. But it is these other walks I would like to dwell upon here.

But first of all I should add that during the nineteenth century – or any century other than our own – to tramp eighty miles along one of Britain's main highways in daily stages was commonplace. Enormous distances were covered by Dorothy and William Wordsworth, and by Coleridge and the Hazlitts – especially Mrs Hazlitt, who was the kind of initial modern woman. She hiked to and fro from Edinburgh to Glasgow during her divorce proceedings, which was a great nuisance to the people carrying them out. Gustav Holst would sometimes walk home to Cheltenham from St. Paul's Girls School, in order to compose. William Langland composed much of *Piers Plowman* whilst on the hoof from Cornhill in London to the Malvern Hills where he was born. Had John Clare been the man he was before disasters of all kinds struck at him, being an inspired walker he would not have been either spiritually daunted or physically wounded by the Great North Road trek: but then he would not have needed to have made it.

His true way, though, was the village footpath. Clare's misfortune was to have some of his favourite paths either ploughed up or straightened out. What we have to appreciate is that part of his personality was as concealment-seeking as the nightingale, as hopefully-hidden as that of certain tucked-away plants on the limestone. The other part was, during his youth at least, like that of any other young man: gregarious, fond of company, of drink and of girls. It was the Clare of the footpaths, and their fugitive destinations, and their hidden bends where he could 'drop down' as he described it to write, to daydream, to have his soul fed by what surrounded him, which produced the poetry. Clare was clearly unaware of how often he mentions footpaths, and his essentially secret wanderings, often just within a stone's throw of the little toiling or playing groups of Helpston itself. Some of his finest footpath writing appears in his essay 'The Woodman, or the Beauties of a Winter Forest'. Here Clare reveals his closest observation, not of birds, but of his footpath-walking neighbours, who are exposed by winter, when all the growth is stripped. There was no cover in winter in the countryside. So he wrote:

> [...] the shepherd cuts his journeys short and now only visits his flock on necessity ... Croodling with his hands in his pockets and his crook under his arm he tramples the frosty plain with dithering haste; glad and eager to return to the warm corner of his cottage fire [...] The milk-boy too in his morning rambles no longer saunters to the pasture as he had used to do in summer (pausing on every pathway flower and swanking idly along, often staring with open mouth thoughtlessly musing on the heavens as if he could wish for something in the passing clouds; leaning his lazy sides 'gainst every stile he come[s] to, and can never get his heavy clouted shoon over the lowest without resting; sighing as he retires with the deepest regret to leave such easy chairs)—But now in hasty claumping tread finding nothing but cold and snow to pause on [...] he wishes for nothing but his journeys end
>
> (*Natural History*, pp.4-5)

At Helpston

In March that same year, 1825, Clare's footpath presents, where he is concerned, sights more vigorous and fascinating, although he is still not entirely alone. We cannot comprehend – I can just remember it as a child – how peopled the countryside was. I went for a walk not long ago, about six miles, and never met a single person in the fields or gardens, and hardly any cars in the narrow lane. But had I walked in my grandfather's time there would be groups of people – hedging, ditching, doing things, children playing, hundreds of people going for walks, courting couples, etc., because the fields really *were* where everybody met. On 25 March, Clare writes:

> I took a walk today to botanize & found that the spring had taken up her dwelling in good earnest she has covered the woods with the white anemonie which the childern call Lady smocks & the hare bells are just venturing to unfold their blue drooping bells the green is covered with daisies & the little Celandine the hedge bottoms are crowded with the green leaves of the arum w[h]ere the boy is peeping for pootys with eager anticipations & delight
>
> (*Natural History*, p.59).

Well, *our* footpaths are either deserted, or protected, or threatened, or deliberately walked on by self-conscious ramblers and others, and many still exist for their original purpose, which was to make bee-lines across the farmland to moors, or along coasts, or to work. And vast numbers exist on local maps, but not in real local knowledge. Many have grown into lanes, and the lanes themselves have grown into roads. A lane is defined as a narrow way between hedges and banks. A footpath is the narrowest way, trodden between crops or wild plants. John Clare mourned the loss of many of them after Helpston was enclosed. Indeed he raged and ranted about it; justly, at what for him was the sacrilege of destroying one of the holiest places in any village: that way along which his people had walked for centuries, a sanctified route to work, a sanctified route to love, a sanctified route to companionship, and to things which were infinitely precious to a man, a woman, or a child.

Some years ago I was taken to Bunyan's footpaths by a friend, and I saw that the site of the great writer's family house was just a rough little cot by the side of a rivulet, which had supplied water for the Bunyans for centuries: nothing there except a few tiles amongst the weeds. The total disappearance of his house excepted, Bunyan's home fields at Elstow must be among the least changed surroundings of any major British author. But they still can only be reached by the footpaths which he used, one of which follows the stream from Harrowden, and the other of which leads to the centre of his village. And – shades of John Clare – the vicar of a neighbouring parish had written that in Anno 1625 (this is when Bunyan was three years old) 'one Bunyan of Elstow, climbing of rook's nests in the Berry Wood, found three rooks in a nest, all as white as milk, and not a black feather in them'.

Footpaths did not guarantee solitude; we make a mistake sometimes to think that Clare by simply walking away from the middle of his village found solitude. There was always somebody up a tree, or under a bush, or just tiffling about, as they used to say, with a scythe, or hiding away with a sweetheart or a book, or usually just routinely travelling to the workplace. Bunyan was a whitesmith who had to carry a heavy anvil on his back to the houses which needed their pewter mended, and he would sensibly have always chosen the narrow way. But it was not a lonely way.

Footpaths may have had to be used by everybody, but they often could only be walked in single file, and should you meet someone coming from the opposite direction you would step into the undergrowth to let them pass. The constant narrow walking seemed to stimulate the wild flowers which separated just far enough to allow human feet to progress. And similarly there were ground nests perilously close to where one walked. I used to know the writer Adrian Bell, who wrote his trilogy in an old farmhouse, just below mine. During the snowy Christmas of 1928, Adrian Bell noted how, due to the lanes being blocked by drifts, the people were seen plodding straight to their objects across the fields, whether it is to the church spire, snow-encrusted cottages, or the chimneys. 'And who are they?', he asks, 'not travellers from afar, for they would not venture out today at all. No, these are the parish workers, who when times are normal, take serpentine routes by by-roads on bicycles'.

At Helpston

'Take the gentle path', advises George Herbert in his plea, 'Discipline'. Bunyan maintained that a simple way to become a heavenly footman – he means a walker in paradise, not a servant—was to walk the earth. Until recently, few had any alternative. Just before this century, everyone walked. Clare's constant walking in his landscape was the norm; except that sometimes he walked, where his Helpston neighbours were concerned, to what was recognisably work – gardening, ploughing, hedging, erranding; and sometimes to what to them was clearly not work – reading and writing, in dips and hollows – a very strange thing to do; and sometimes he walked just to look. And so he became what most village people dread being: odd, strange, different. With so many of the hereditary footpaths over-exposed by enclosure, Clare walked on, until he himself was mercifully enclosed by the woods and the wilds, and by the useless waste at Barnack, where the plough could not go in. These remote and, in summertime especially, overgrown footpaths became his dreamlines.

He often writes of dropping down, a kind of birdlike movement, when some thought strikes him, in order to make a note of it. When he was working as a lime-burner, he had to walk between two kilns which were about three miles apart, one at Pickworth and one at Ryhall. At Pickworth, he worked with another man; at Ryhall, by himself, and he wrote:

> ...I often went there to work by myself w[h]ere I had leisure to study over such things on my journeys of going and returning to and fro; and on these walks morning and night I have dropd down 5 or 6 times, to [write] (*By Himself*, p.22)

There was no dropping down when he was ploughing, which is a very public thing to do. What came to him in the fields he had to hold tight in his head, after a day's toiling on the farm, until he got to his bedroom, then he would write. In his autobiography, Clare uses the walk metaphor to describe his early sense of being both different and isolated. His mother had talked of his going into service, at which he winced, and had given him a box for his things when he left home. All servants left home with a box. But he filled his box with books, and his first poems, and he wrote:

Solvitur Ambulando

> I always looked sullen when my mother talkd of Service [...] I now began to value my abilitys as superiour to my companions and exulted over it in secret ... I considerd walking in the track of others [but] this had as little merit in it as a child walking in leading strings ere it can walk by itself   when I happend with them [i.e. his companions] in my sunday Walks I often try'd their taste by pointing out some striking beauty in a wild flower or object in the surrounding s[c]enery to which they woud seldom make an answer, and if they did twas such as 'they coud see nothing worth looking at' ... I often wondered that, while I was peeping about and finding such quantitys of pleasing things to stop and pause over, another shoud pass me as carless as if he was blind   I thought somtimes that I surely had a taste peculialy by myself and that nobody else thought or saw things as I did
>
> (*By Himself* pp.16-17)

They didn't, of course – until Clare had turned these observations into poems, and then they did. But 'peeping', 'secret', 'seeing', 'finding': this is the language of the footpath walker. Clare's first poem was called 'The Morning Walk' and it was composed while walking to Glinton, two miles. Years later, when he was working on the great book that never was, his Helpston version of White's *Natural History of Selborne*, he remembered a marvellous sight from a footpath, and wrote:

> once when I was young man on staying late at a feast I cross<ed> a meadow about midnight & saw to my supprise quantitys of small nimble things emigrating across it a long way from any water I thought at first that they were snakes but I found on a closer observation that ther were young eels making for a large pond called the Islet pool which they journeyd to with as much knowledge as if they were acquainted with the way I thought this a wonderfull discovery
>
> (*Natural History*, pp.69-70)

Clare was more than acquainted with the way, that simplest, purest, most eloquent of ways, the footpath. And life only went wrong when he was diverted from it. He knew where he stood. He

At Helpston

knew where he should walk. He knew when he should drop down. He knew what no other English writer knew or knows, which is what the English countryman's eyes saw, or sees, in its purity. Clare was hard on the 'clowns', as he called them, but we know that countless people, whilst on the way to work, or at work itself, are unwittingly visionary, and that they do not pass through these scenes on earth without taking them in, and wondering at them sometimes. What they, or few of us do, is to drop down in our tracks to write because the need to write is overwhelming, as it is with writers. There were days when Clare could not follow the footpaths. On Thursday 23 September, 1824 he writes:

> A wet day did nothing but nurse my illness Coud not have walkd out had it been fine very disturbd in conscience about the troubles of being forcd to endure life & dye by inches & the anguish of leaving my childern & the dark porch of eternity whence none returns to tell the tale of their reception   (*Natural History*, p.181)

But a few weeks later—what a change!

> Sunday 31 Oct 1824
> Took a walk got some branches of the spindle tree with its pink colord berys that shine beautifully in the pale sun—found for the first time 'the herb true love' or 'one berry' [*Paris quatrifolia*] in Oxey Wood brought a root home to set in my garden
>   (*Natural History*, p.197)

The following Spring, we have endless footpath walks: one at three o'clock in the morning; and one that ended up with the comic scene of Clare barking like a dog to see off a vixen (13 May 1825):

> Met with an extrodinary incident to day while Walking in Open wood to hunt a Nightingales nest – I popt unawares on an old Fox & her four young Cubs that were playing about she saw me & instantly approachd towards me growling like an angry dog I had no stick & tryd all I coud to fright her by imitating the bark of a fox hound

which only irritated her the more & if I had not retreated a few paces back she woud have seized me when I set up an haloo she started
(*Natural History*, p.239)

He had all the countryman's terror of spooks, of shadows, of following footsteps, of fierce animals:

> The boy returning home at night from toil
> Down lane and close oer footbrig gate and style
> Oft trembles into fear and stands to hark
> The waking fox renew his short gruff bark
> While badgers eccho their dread evening shrieks
> And to his thrilling thoughts in terror speaks
> (*Shepherd's Calendar*, 'March', ll. p.170-6)

As Margaret Grainger has pointed out, many of John Clare's walks were systematic. He often wandered, but there were times when he walked to plan. She traces three walks: a walk due east from Northborough, to the River Welland and up the west bank to Deeping Gate; a walk from Nine Bridges, Northborough, along the north bank of the North Drain to Lolham Bridges; and a walk between Waldram Hall and Welland Ford (*Natural History,* p.328). These were systematic walks for work purposes, such as naturalists walk. She also saw signs on some manuscripts which showed that many natural history notes must have been jotted down as he walked, just as he used to do as a young man, when he says 'I usd to drop down behind a hedge bush or dyke and write down my things upon the crown of my hat' (*By Himself*, p.78).

And this also reminds me of the youthful Thomas Hardy. I had to help edit the new Wessex edition of Hardy in the 1970s, and read a lot about his work methods (writers are always fascinated by other writers' work methods, even down to ink and pens, and where they sat). I went to Bockhampton, the thatched birthplace, near Dorchester, and into the room he shared with his brother. There was a little cupboard where they kept their clothes, and there was the narrow wooden window-seat in a casement, on which Hardy sat to

At Helpston

write *Far From the Madding Crowd*. The house had been built by his grandfather, in a woodland – the woodland of *The Woodlanders* in fact – and when Hardy needed to stretch his legs he would dash out of the cottage and go for a walk where the woodlanders were working: with axes, not chainsaws. When you cut a tree down two men axe it in alternative strokes and white chippings fly out. Thinking of something new to put in *The Woodlanders* Hardy would pick up the chips and write on them, place them in his pockets, take them home and fit them into the chapter. Clare too was doing this kind of thing when he used his hat as a desk. Both writers shared this u rgency to put things down.

References to his footpath walks to both of his kinds of work, on the farms and on the page, are myriad in Clare's poetry. In 'Stray Walks' he says:

> How pleasant are the fields to roam and think
> Whole sabbaths through, unnoticed and alone
> *(Middle Period*, IV, p.302)

And there is the ever-sacred walk to Mary Joyce, the walk he took when he could no longer walk alone. One of the horrible ironies of Clare's life was that he, the walker, was incarcerated for so long (it is one thing to walk on footpaths, and quite another to walk in the grounds of an asylum, or even to Northampton Church). The sacred walk to Mary Joyce went on many years after the courtship: it went on at Northborough, at Epping, and at Northampton. He wrote:

> I've ran the furlongs to thy door
> And thought the way as miles
> With doubts that I should see thee not
> And scarcely staid for stiles
> (Summerfield, p.133)

And he wrote:

> Past stiles the which a steeple we espy

Solvitur Ambulando

>Peeping stretching in the distant sky
>>('Pleasant Places', *Selected Poems and Prose*, p.160)

(That is *Glinton* of course).

I will conclude with that masterpiece of footpath observation, 'The Pewits Nest'. As we read Clare we recognise the poetry of a walking man. It touches us because we are all descended from the walking men, the walking women, the walking children: and not so very long ago either. Sometimes we forget that it wasn't only the poets, and novelists like Hardy, who had these wonderful ideas as they walked. *Solvitur ambulando* was for all of us, because it stimulates (I don't know whether jogging does that: I rather doubt it). Certainly, these long walks to work, these long walks to school, these long walks with a friend, these long walks just to get out of the house, etc., were part of the pattern of the life of people right up until the modern age. And whilst it happened, their minds ticked over in an extraordinary way. Because men and women haven't all been able to write, or paint, or make music about certain things, it doesn't mean they haven't experienced them – this is a common mistake. When Crabbe was writing his extremely critical descriptions of *The Village* and *The Borough* he always maintained, and made great care, to sort a few individuals from among the sullen inhabitants who, although ordinary fishermen, fieldworkers, and so on, were also ornithologists, collected butterflies, made gardens, knew about marsh flowers and other things. These were the kind of people Clare used to meet. We call them self-educated, but their true education is not something we can comprehend. It was far deeper than the reading of a few books. It was the landscape being articulated in their heads, via their normal work practices. They had to work long hours. They didn't live as long as we live, but they often saw things as much as poets see things. But they didn't write them down. We cannot possibly sum up what happened long ago, we can only accept and know what artists and writers have taught us. The social historian now travels these paths.

Here is a walking poem, called 'The Pewits Nest':

At Helpston

Accross the fallow clods at early morn
I took a random track, where scant and spare
The grass and nibbled leaves all closely shorn
Leaves a burnt flat all bleaching brown and bare
Where hungry sheep in freedom range forlorn
And 'neath the leaning willow and odd thorn
And molehill large that vagrant shade supplies
They batter round to shun the teazing flies
Trampling smooth places hard as cottage floors
Where the time-killing lonely shepherd boys
Whose summer homes are ever out of doors
Their chockholes form and chalk their marble ring
And make their clay taws at the bubbling spring
And in their rangling sport and gambling joys
They straine their clocklike shadows—when it cloys
To guess the hour that slowly runs away
And shorten sultry turmoil with their play
   Here did I roam while veering overhead
The pewet whirred in many whewing rings
And 'chewsit' screamed and clapped her flapping wings.
To hunt her nest my rambling steps was led
O'er the broad baulk beset with little hills
By moles long-formed and pismires tennanted
As likely spots—but still I searched in vain
When all at once the noisey birds were still
And on the lands a furrowed ridge between
Chance found four eggs of dingy dirty green
Deep-blotched with plashy spots of jockolate stain
Their small ends inward turned as ever found
As though some curious hand had laid them round
Yet lying on the ground with nought at all
Of soft grass withered twitch and bleached weed
To keep them from the rain storms' frequent fall
And here she broods on her unsavory bed
When bye and bye with little care and heed
Her young with each a shell upon its head

Solvitur Ambulando

Run after their wild parents' restless cry
And from their own fears' tiney shadows run
'Neath clods and stones to cringe and snugly lie
Hid from all sight but the all-seeing sun
Till never – ceasing danger seemeth bye
    (*Middle Poems*, III, p.472)

The green woodpecker, 1986

THE POET AND THE NEST

We can do some writers no greater injustice than to read them primarily for the information of their times. John Clare is constantly in danger of such readings. But those inventories of his were made for his own peace of mind, not our education, although the bird lists, reminders for him, remind us, quite unbearably, of the wonderful *Natural History of Helpstone* that never was. When we read his inventories we see a totting-up of what he refused to believe he had lost – and we see everything which, as twenty-first century country people, we once possessed. For a great many of us are in direct descent from John Clare's landworkers. He leaves little out. He was making his lists at the very moment in agricultural history when there were for the first time more people in the factories than on the farms. He would not have known this. For Clare field toil would have gone on and on until kingdom come. The huge changes he witnessed, the coming of the railway, enclosure, some mechanisation on the surrounding estates, he treated as unwanted disturbances to the old hard way of life which had for him a spiritual quality of such importance that to alter it was a blasphemy. He was for ever counting what it consisted of right down to the honeydew on the sycamores, to a boy's song, to Mrs Nottingham of the Exeter Arms' description of fifteen will-o-the-wisps dancing reels on Eastwell Moor. Nothing was left out, from the footsteps of girls to the shouts of shepherds, from the insect on the stalk to the sound of those same bells which we hear today.

Helpston was no Eden – Clare was never clearer than on this point – but it was his. Illness and the powers that be took it from him, or would have done so had he not found a way to take it with him. What is the most repeated, most closely observed, most loved centre of his 'belonging' in his poetry and prose? It is the nest, its secrecy, its intimacy. What is the object of men's ritual discovery and theft? It is the nest. What brought John Clare into stillness and contemplation,

The Poet and the Nest

into a silence in which he could hear his heart beating? It was the nest with its sitting bird. His finding and, watching nests, took him through folklore, botany and ornithology into a profound self-discovery. Hence that superb list of nest poems which, whilst giving us such unique observations of nature, give us something extra, the poet in all his strength and song and vulnerability. 'The Fern Owls Nest', 'The Ravens Nest', 'The Moorhens Nest', 'The Pewits Nest', 'The Robins Nest' and, finest of all, 'The Nightingales Nest', these nervous, furtive but complete observations are unique in literature. There is nothing like them.

Bird's-nesting was until quite recently a tolerated activity for country boys. Pity, courage – some nests were high – and competition drove it. It was kind to take a single egg whilst the mother bird bravely screamed a foot or two above. The egg was sucked or blown and placed with many others in a cotton-wool drawer, the rarer the better. Seamus Heaney writes of 'boy-deeds' and recalls a particularly daring boy-deed by Michael Collins, a man born to be king or president. As a boy he made a practice of coming down the chute with the hay whirling from a high loft to the ground in a cloud of dried flowers and grass. Later on, says Heaney, Collins was ambushed in the Pass of Flowers, shot down, having nothing to hold on to.

John Clare was in free-fall all his life. The various and many helping hands held out to save him proved useless. Eventually they caught him and put him in a cage. Here he went on singing, lyrically, sadly, satirically, nostalgically. None of those who shared his cage get a mention, only those who continued to live in the freedom of Helpston, many of whom were in the churchyard, or who he translated to his other native place, Scotland.

Clare's early boy-deeds had to double with child labour, the latter being the custom and the reality. At eight he was wielding a toy-sized flail in the stone barn alongside Parker, his father, though stopping now and then to draw algebraic signs in the killing dust. A pleasant thing happened when he was about ten. Francis Gregory, the young innkeeper next door, got him to run errands and to help plough and reap his eight acres or so of corn. Francis was unmarried and lived with his mother at the Blue Bell. They were both ill. Looking back, Clare

At Helpston

said, 'They used me uncommon well as if I was their own'. Mother and son lie by the church tower, their helper by the chancel wall. However, continued Clare, ''Tis irksome to a boy to be alone and he is ready in such situations to snatch hold of any trifle to divert his loss of company, and make up for pleasanter amusements'. Birds-nesting in the ordinary way would have topped these amusements, but Clare, in his autobiographical *Sketches*, confesses to a very different pastime. It was that there, in Francis Gregory's cornfield, he began his 'muttering', his softly speaking aloud of the rhymes which he would later write down in his bedroom, a tile shifted to let in light. He would memorise lines as he walked to and from Maxey Mill, lugging flour. Boys sang, they did not mutter, and eyes would have been upon him, this child talking to himself, a sure sign of something being wrong. Or different, which is not a good thing to be.

And all this before a Methodist friend loaned him that fragment of James Thomson's famous poem *The Seasons*. The other day I found an ancient anthology entitled *Poetry of the Year, 1867* and in it, only three years after Clare's death, were scattered among work by Crabbe, Bloomfield, Burns and others six poems by him. And what lines introduce this collection? None other than those which introduced Clare to poetry: Thomson's:

> Come, gentle spring, etherial mildness, come,
> And from the bosom of yon dropping cloud,
> While music wakes around, veiled in a shower
> Of shadowing roses, on our plains descend.

The editor would not have known this. Serendipity had him by the hand. The electric words for Clare would have been 'our plains'. Both Thomson and he were lowlanders, singers of the levels. Something else appeared to have left a memorable mark at this youthful moment, for Clare makes it an important point in the *Sketches*. It concerned his arrangement with the kind Gregorys at the Blue Bell – it was 'The only year I lived in hired service in my life'. He mentions it because of it being all too close to his mother's plan to put him into domestic service. She had already got him a box for his clothes. He filled it with books.

Francis Gregory, the former-publican, and Clare shared a friend named John Turnill who helped the jobbing boy with his maths. It was Turnill who composed the lines for Gregory's tombstone under the tower.

I thought of John Turnill when we were exploring Robert Bloomfield's countryside near Thetford only to discover that the churchyard of his patron Capel Lofft had been recently vandalised for the sake of the lawnmower, the memorials pulled up and made into paths and a rockery, their tender village verses under our feet. Nineteenth century funerary verse may not be Wordsworth but it might well be Turnill or some other young man mourning his friend.

Robert Bloomfield was still a child when farmwork was thought too heavy for him, so they sent him to a London den to learn shoemaking. A similar fate awaited John Clare before the landlord of the Blue Bell took him in. Is this pub named after Scotland's harebell or *Endymion non-scriptus* – without the Greek 'Ai!' which can be seen in the throat of narcissus, that cry of despair? Bluebells were once the most picked flower in the English woods.

Margaret Grainger in her *Natural History Prose Writings of John Clare* sees him always doubling his boy-deeds, his 'watching of the night-jar was an inextricable part of his late night wanderings for courting purposes – he had been a lover since he was fourteen – and his searching for ferns accompanied his efforts to throw off ill health'. He becomes an expert on cover, learning this essential art – Helpston always had its eye on him – from the birds. 'The Mavis thrush', like himself at this moment, 'sings like the song of a young bird while learning to sing'. Like him, 'It loves to frequent ... old orchards and hedge borders ... near the village with a song [in December] when it can get shelter and cover as if it loved to treat the village with a song at such a dreary season. [But] as the spring advances its song ceases and it disappears to its more solitary haunts of woods and forests where it builds its nest beside a large tree on the twigs and water grains that shoot from the body. Its nest is made of the blades of dead grass moss and cowdung lined with warmer materials of wool and a finer sort of grass ... The Mavis never forgets her dead ramping grass [couch grass] for the out side covering and a plentiful supply of wool within the wool is what bird nesting boys know it bye'.

At Helpston

In Clare's *Biographys of Birds*, one of my favourite book titles and his *Bird List* which he made for the tantalising *Natural History of Helpstone*, birds' nests stretch out like an ornithological city. The Large Wood Owle, by which Clare possibly means the tawny owl, 'attacks boys in a bold manner', the Raven builds where it is difficult to climb, the jackdaw in uninhabited houses, and as to magpies which sway about in nests filled with teaspoons, well they are apt to keep their loot. It horrifies him to see the overseers of Helpston rewarding boys who kill sparrows and he would give:

> To tyrant boys a fee
> To buy the captive sparrows liberty

As he wrote in his poem 'The Fate of Genius'. The fate of genius in the villages of his day could be quite terrifying. So hide away, hide away. Take Cover. Find cover on 'our plain':

> Boys thread the woods
> To their remotest shades
> But in these marshy flats, these stagnant floods,
> Security pervades.
>
> From year to year
> Places untrodden lie
> Where man nor boy nor stock ventured near
> – Naught gazed on but the sky
>
> And fowl that dread
> The very breath of man
> Hiding in spots that never knew his tread
> A wild and timid clan
>
> In these thy haunts
> I've gleaned habitual love
> From the vague world where pride and folly taunts
> I muse and look above

The Poet and the Nest

> Thy solitudes
> The unbounded heaven esteems
> And here my heart warms into higher moods
> And dignifying dreams

Clare often turns to nests which lie on the ground and sometimes finds them safest. He himself feels secure in lying low. Fame elevated him and hurt him, and he was sighted by the spoilers. In the sequence of nest poems, among the greatest natural history poems in the language, he finds a metaphor for his happiness and his plight. They are a miracle of close observation, both of himself treading carefully and of a sitting bird such as the peewit brooding 'on her unsavoury nest', and of moorhens on their safe 'shelved nests'. The accuracy of the descriptions result from many lengthy scarcely-daring-to-breathe starings at building material, delicate eggs and parent birds which were not conscious of the poet's presence. These observations reach perfection in 'The Nightingales Nest', which tells of Clare's nest-finding apprenticeship and, after many boyish attempts at birdwatching, that it needed maturity for him to come close. It is then that he witnesses those connections which touch his own existence.

> How curious is the nest no other bird
> Uses such loose materials or weaves
> Their dwellings in such spots – dead oaken leaves
> Are placed without and velvet moss within
> And little scraps of grass – and scant and spare
> Of what seems scarce materials down and hair
> Far from mans haunts she seemeth naught to win
> Yet nature is the builder and contrives
> Homes for her childerns comfort even here
> Where solitudes deciples spend their lives...

Clare's nest was robbed of him, shaken to bits and had to be reconstructed in his head. Taken from the nest, he joined those who sang the great songs of exile.

A weasel moving its young from loose straw to baled straw and back again

CLARE'S TWO HUNDRETH BIRTHDAY

In Helpston Parish Church

Ghosts cannot blush, but if the shade of that small figure who knew this ancient interior is present, then it will be startled by the warmth of our feelings and the depth of our admiration. He would have remembered not only his own birthday but that of his twin sister. It was she who they believed would survive. Clare obliges us to shed whatever intellectual trappings we possess when, once a year, we journey to his village to talk and walk where his circumscribed yet boundary-less life was lived. We are in a little world writ large because of the great things he found here, and it becomes a condition of our being able to come close to him to recover our own simplicity. He is in a sense our common ancestor, for the majority of us have family trees rooted in farms and fields. John Clare tells us who and what we were not so very long ago by giving a full account of who he was, a gift which, as we know, cost him his freedom and his necessary joys.

Thoughts on John Clare on his bi-centenary, thoughts which were given an extra stimulus when I found myself reading a tiny book containing some of William Barnes's poems sent to me by my old friend J.L. Carr. Maybe he is here with us at this moment so that I can tell him yet again, modest writer that he is, that he is a master of the conte, that difficult form of the long short-story. But some twenty years ago he began to issue from his Kettering press a series of small literary maps and selections which acted like bait, so that I and all his readers were soon swallowing, William Barnes, for instance. The Barnes volume, if one can call it that, arrived when I was helping to edit the New Wessex edition of the Works of Thomas Hardy. In it I read the matchless 'Linden Lea', 'Woak Hill' and 'Wife a-Lost'. John Clare was eight when Barnes was born and there is little or no evidence to show that either poet knew anything of the other's existence. And yet

At Helpston

each dealt with the persistent sadness of rural life, with that indefinable melancholy which is so large a part of 'feeling', and so less a part of 'condition'. Robert Bridges, who had once written Barnes off in a letter to Gerard Manley Hopkins, received a sharp reply. 'I hold your contemptuous opinion a mistake. Barnes is a perfect artist. It is as if Dorset Life and Landscape had taken flesh and blood in the man'. We now know that two of England's greatest poets, Hopkins and Hardy, were in a sense taught by Barnes. Similarly, we also know that all rural writing has taken flesh and blood from John Clare. Geoffrey Grigson said that Barnes sent his work to the local newspaper and, other than paste his cuttings into a home-made brown paper album, forgot all about it. 'I wrote them, so to say, as if I could not well help it, the writing of them was not work but like the playing of music'.

He also wrote them in the Dorset dialect, which sent the anthology editors, when they came to them, wild. Why the local speech, so accurately caught and written down, yet surely so limiting? Because only it could capture the sadness and the tenderness of the field people and, as with Clare, the enormity of displacement. In 'Woak Hill' a widower and his children and the furniture are moving to another cottage, and he is careful to put out his hand to lead his wife's ghost to it. Her name was Mary. E.M. Forster said that if one read this poem without tears—then one had not succeeded in reading it. And Hardy said that '"Woak Hill" has been matched by few singers below the best'. If I was an English teacher, I would add, 'Compare with John Clare's "The Flitting". Observe the spiritual upheaval of the short village house-move and learn what once shook the family soul.'

Due to the long asylum years Clare missed out on some of the contacts he might have made with some of the rural writers of the mid-nineteenth century. But then so did Barnes and Hopkins, and where his poetry was concerned, so did Thomas Hardy, all of whose work in this respect received an essentially twentieth century recognition. Our essential duty is not to read Clare for his copious sociology, natural history and linguistics alone, endlessly instructive though he is, but as the major poet of the English village. Today of all days is when we have to hear what he meant us to hear. His restless pencil and scratchy pen would sometimes have been at work in this church and in the lane outside. All in all he was writing about those big mistakes which we all make, those losses which we all suffer, about the guilty bliss of being alone, about desire, about seesawing craziness and levelheadedness, about friendship, about women and sex, about plodding along in some dull furrow. About the glory of birds and flowers. He is far nearer to us than time will admit.

Coleridge, whom Clare once met, defending the language in which he and Wordsworth wrote *Lyrical Ballads*, objected to rural speech being called 'the *real* language of Men'. He said, 'I object in the very first instance to an equivocation in the use of the word "real". Every man's language varies according to the extent of his knowledge, the activity of his faculties, and the depth and quickness of his feelings. For "real" therefore, we must substitute ordinary *lingua communis*. And this is no more to be found in the phraseology of low and rustic life than in any other class.' Scholars here today have revealed the extent of Clare's knowledge, where natural history was concerned equal if different to that of many professionals of his time. But all he knew and understood is subsumed in poetry. That Helpston recognised this is made plain in Greg Crossan's full and enthralling accounts of Clare's funeral here on 25th May 1864 and the first centennial celebration of July 1893, which were both comprehending of his genius and lavish in their pride and affection. Yet during his lifetime we know that his 'right to song' was constantly undermined by helpers and critics alike, troubling him deeply and contributing to his 'shipwreck'. But as we also know, his muse remained unquestioning and unfailing.

The demoiselles, 1983

SIGNPOSTS

My first reading would almost certainly have been 'Little Trotty Wagtail'. Where I went from there I can't remember but I expect it would have been to Edmund Blunden's *Sketches in the Life of John Clare by Himself* (1931) in which I encountered that spare existence with a certain familiarity, for the English village had not altered that much between the wars. Blunden was a neighbour and when after the First World War he began the process of Clare's rehabilitation his address was 'Belle Vue, Stansfield, Clare, Suffolk'. Those who worked the fields around his cottage during that terrible hard-up time did so in conditions almost as harsh as those in Clare's lifetime. I remember Blunden coming to read Clare at our local literary society and his giving me all his notes, and his certainty of John Clare's greatness. There is a delightful vignette of Blunden in his first-recognition-of-John Clare days in Siegfried Sassoon's diary.

> 16th June 1922. I left here early on Monday morning, and reached Clare station about 12.30. From Liverpool Street to Mark's Tey ... It was a sunshiny day, and there was little Blunden waiting for me in his shabby blue suit. He had just picked up a first edition of *Atalanta in Calydon* for a shilling in a little shop in Clare. And outside the station sat Mary B. in a smart blue cloak, in a tiny ramshackle wagonette drawn by a small white pony ... And for three days B. and I talked about county cricket, and the war and English poetry and our own poetry and East Anglia and our contemporaries ... And B. wrote reviews, and I read Clare and Bloomfield and Blunden ...

It was Blunden who was the first person I had ever met who had been to Helpston.

A perennial question when Clare is mentioned is, 'Where did he get it from?' His own parents were among the first to ask it, and almost

At Helpston

everybody since. Tennyson asked it in connection with Keats – 'He had a touch, and yet he was a livery stable keeper's son. I don't know where he got it from, unless from Heaven!' Where did Tennyson get it from? Not from Trinity College, Cambridge. We may smile but it was the implication that Clare possessed what his kind shouldn't have which helped to make him ill. In his little autobiography he hazards, as any writer might do, 'where he got it from'. From his kind teacher at Glinton, from 'my reading of books', from 'the fine Hebrew poem of Job', from a tale called *Zig-Zag*, from five lines by Thomson, from the accident of his Scottish blood, from views of Northamptonshire which neither the locals nor the tourists would ever be able to see with their own eyes. In short, from a little education and his own limitless observation. A few months after Clare's death a student copied some of his poetry into his diary. The student was Gerard Manley Hopkins. This is the way poetry travels. In this way Clare has never been neglected or lost or in need of discovery, and a tracing of his influence from Hopkins to Ted Hughes would spring some surprises. Yet for the full picture of him and the magnitude of his achievement we shall for ever be indebted to the work of a group of today's scholars whose skill is beginning to reveal both Clare and his countryside with ever fresh insights. Our Society could claim to be Britain's most environment-conscious literary group. If, as Clare confessed, he kicked the poetry out of the clods, we now recognise as earlier generations could never have done the wonders which make up a lump of soil. There were times when he wished that earth had remained simply earth as the farm labourers saw it. Asked at the Epping asylum which he liked best, 'literature or your former vocation?' he replied, 'I like hard work best. I was happy then. Literature has destroyed my head and brought me here.' And yet, as we know from the remarkable output of the long asylum years, it would be the writer who would ultimately prevail. Just as Clare had the power to articulate the life of the fields and common lands with a reality unknown to any previous English poet, so did he articulate the common disaster of so many country people of his day who through penury, age or mental illness were packed into workhouse and madhouse. And yet in his work one is in constant encounter with joy, something he knew more about than almost anything else. It is his puzzle. The other thing he knows all about is the bliss of the hidden life. In days of despair he would write of the shipwreck of all he was but regularly throughout his life there would always be this sometimes snug, sometimes exquisite satisfaction of possessing either a love or an existence of which he could never be robbed. It shows in some of the poems which Seamus Heaney and Ted Hughes have included in their happily indulgent anthology *The Rattle Bag*, in his song 'I hid my love', for instance which, although a trail of farewells and absences, is also a triumphant account of the privacy of the heart. It was hard for anyone not to be under constant observation in what was essentially a gregarious late-Georgian village and one of the delights of reading Clare is to accompany him to his hides.

One of the most tantalising 'what might have beens' of Clare's life, and one I have often referred to over the years, was the inconclusive natural history of his countryside which Hessey the publisher suggested, directing him to Gilbert White's now celebrated *Natural History and Antiquities of Selborne*. It was a percipient suggestion, far more so than Hessey could have realised at the time. But it was accompanied with such warnings as 'prose may injure your Poetical Name', and at a time when Clare's confidence was being undermined by editors, none of whom were capable of recognising his unique indigenous scientific qualifications, as it were, for describing his native heath, his wide reading, his accurate eye, above all his passion for everything which grew, flew, ran or simply was. He himself was a partly wild creature when seen in the terms of village society and was half-trapped and half-released by being a once acclaimed poet. Although he had lovers, friends and neighbours, his easiest and fullest communication was with Nature. When a naturalist went to see Thomas Hardy, then at the peak of his fame, he was disconcerted to discover that 'he did not know the flowers of the field'. Nor did, or do, most country people. But Clare knew them both botanically and emotionally. He shared their habitat. He too grew there. Transplanted, he lost his necessary light. Margaret Grainger in her *Natural History Prose Writings of John Clare* rightly says that had Hessey and all the rest of them shown a bit more faith in him, Helpston might now possess a similar reputation to that of Selborne.

At Helpston

Here is a sample of what might have been from one of the Natural History Letters which Clare wrote to James Hessey. It is about the Landrail and the Quail, birds which were endowed with wonder for the would-be Northamptonshire Gilbert White.

> W[h]ere is the school boy that has not heard that mysterious noise which comes with the spring in the grass & green corn I have followd it for hours & all to no purpose it seemd like a spirit that mockd my folly in running after it... About two years ago while I was walking in a neighbours homstead we heard one of these landrails in his wheat we hunted down the land & accidentily as it were we stirted it up it seemd to flye very awkard & its long legs hung down as if they were broken it was just at dewfall in the evening it flew towards the street instead of the field & popt into a chamber window that happend to be open when a cat seizd & killd it it was somthing like the quail but smaller & very slender with no tail scarcly & rather long legs it was of a brown color they lay like the quail & partridge upon the ground in the corn & grass they make no nest but scrat a hole in the ground & lay a great number of eggs My mother found a landrails nest once while weeding wheat with seventeen eggs & they were not sat on they were short eggs made in the form of the partridges but somthing smaller staind with large spots of a dark color not much unlike the color of the plovers I imagine the young run with 'the shells on their heads'... The quail is almost as much of a mystery in the summer landscape & comes with the green corn like the [landrail] tho it is seen more often & is more easily urgd to take wing it makes an odd noise in the grass as if it said 'wet my foot wet my foot' which Weeders & Haymakers hearken to as a prophecy of rain...   (*Natural History*, pp.49-50)

Clare began to keep his *A Natural History of Helpstone* (sub-titled *Biographys of Birds and Flowers*) in September 1824. Only a month later he became ill and upset. Young villagers were sick and dying. The old rural life was marked by sudden spates of pain and mortality through tuberculosis or fevers. Clare draws his own tombstone in his Journal and reveals how depressed he is by finding 'three fellows at the end of Royce wood who I found were laying out the plan for an "Iron rail way'" (*Natural History*, p.245). And yet, as Margaret Grainger says, these fears and miseries are written down at the same time as a mass of poems, a reading list which reveals hours of pleasure and the records of many fascinating excursions in the company of the sympathetic Billings brothers, the learned Edmund Artis and Joseph Henderson, the head gardener who seemed to know everything, especially how to cheer up depressed genius. Clare knows that his response to many of the things which get him down is irrational – and even anti-village – and he acknowledges this with charm and honesty. Here he is in the same mood as Gerard Manley Hopkins when he saw what had been done to the poplars at Binsey.

> – my two favourite Elm trees at the back of the hut are condemned to dye it shocks me to relate it but tis true the savage who owns them thinks they have done their best & now he wants to make use of the benefits he can get from selling them... I have been several mornings to bid them farewell – had I £100 to spare I would buy their reprieves – but they must dye – yet this mourning over trees is all foolishness they feel no pains they are but wood cut up or not... was People all to feel & think as I do the world coud not be carried on – a green woud not be ploughd a tree or bush woud not be cut for firing or furniture & every thing they found when boys would remain in that state until they dyd – this is my indisposition & you will laugh at it – (*Letters*, p.161)

I shall end this piecing together of presidential fragments with what I can recall of the talk I gave on Clare's recurring theme of boyhood, chiefly his own but also village boyhood generally. The persistence of this theme was part-deliberate, part-unconscious. He had not only to record it, but to constantly re-imagine it. Later he would use it to combat what he called 'this sad non-identity.' The first thing which any writer has to discover is who he is. Clare had regularly to remind himself who he was. This is not only the fate of madmen, or of poets like Coleridge, who would never do after thirty what he had done during his twenties, but of us all to some degree.

John Clare was not a visionary, he was a remembrancer. He remembers his father's pride: 'Boy, who could have thought, when we

At Helpston

were threshing together some years back, thou wouldst thus be noticed, and be enabled to make us all thus happy?' He remembers the darkening of the original scene, how 'All that map of boyhood was overcast' by Enclosure, how his first and only complete love was 'thwarted', he remembers himself aged ten asking, 'Who owns the land?' He remembers what few poets remember, the exuberance of children. His work rings with the voices of noisy labouring young people. *The Shepherd's Calendar* is full of singing, shouting, whistling and general hubbub, of calling and cries. There is the happy dirty driving boy, the bawling herdboy, the fanciful shepherd's boy, the talkative boy at the shearing, the loud bird-scaring boy, all of them, and countless girls besides, briefly, enchantingly wild – until

> Reason like a winter's day
> Nipt childhood's visions all away.
> Those truths are fled and left behind
>   A real world & a doubting mind.

John Clare, of course did not have his childhood visions nipt away, hence his achievement, hence his suffering, hence his dilemma. In full possession of them until the end of his life, he could only make use of them. His constant refrain, 'when I was a boy', is always a reminder that he is going to say something which is far from childish. 'When I was a boy I used to be very curious to watch the nightingale.' The word 'watch' instead of 'hear' or 'listen to' is a revelation. 'When I was a boy there was a little spring of beautiful soft water which was never dry. It used to dribble its way through the grass in a little ripple of its own making, no bigger than a grip or cart-rut. And in this little springhead there used to be hundreds of little fish called a minnow. We used to go on Sunday in harvest to leck [bail] it out with a dish and string the fish on rushes...thinking ourselves great fishers.' His recollection of this fecund scene, when placed alongside his memory of the same area after it had been drastically rationalised by the new agricultural policy sounds all too familiar to late twentieth-century ears.

Signposts

> Inclosure like a Buonaparte let not a thing remain
> It levelled every bush and tree and levelled every hill
> And hung the moles for traitors – though the brook is running still
> It runs a naked stream cold and chill
> (from 'Remembrances')

But Clare's real indictment of what the Georgian planners did to Helpston is about the destruction of its hides. Not only he the poet, but every village child needed a mesh of heaths, muddles, ancient stretches of no-man's land, personal footpaths, dells and warrens. This was where from time immemorial boys grew up. It was Clare's university, where he read, where he thought, where he watched, and most of all where he could disappear. When he was small it was exciting to have a barn all to himself on Sundays. His first writings, he tells us, were made in barn-dust.

The home ground of many writers casts a familiar spell. The home ground of John Clare which I, and most members of the Society, see for a day a year, is more the actual seed-ground of a remarkable literature than perhaps any other corner of England. We, of course, will have to take care not to become more absorbed in the place, time and conditions which created it than in the poetry itself.

Magpie flying up from a wet road

SILENT LIKENESS

My first statue stood on Market Hill, Sudbury, Suffolk. It was of Thomas Gainsborough in his prime and when the great artist was pitched above the noisy market stalls in a stance of supreme achievement. He stared across to his birthplace a few yards west, palette and brush at the ready. His clothes were beautiful and in winter he changed them for a suit of glittering white. The corporation lights swung above him and we locals milled around him, pleased that an Australian sculptor and an America donor had wished him on us in 1912. Our little borough had provided him with weather – warped trees, crumbling banks, thin peasants, and pert girls in tight shiny stays. Later he would move on to Ipswich for country squires and parsons, to Bath for the beau monde and Pall Mall for the royals, although taking with him everywhere scraps of where he came from, broken woods, a hut, patches of burdock, a stretch of blue sky, a church tower which to this day no-one can identify. As a boy I felt rather possessive about him. The sculptor had copied his self-portraits and caught, I thought, his quizzical face to a T. Caught just what I wanted to see.

John Clare had an open, unguarded face, Trouble would pass across it like a cloud then leave it clear, as with all visionaries. It is open to us in three forms, a bronze bust, an oil painting and a photograph, added to which we have Edward Drury's candid description of him to John Taylor, written on 20 April 1819:

> Clare canot reason: he writes and can give no reason for using a fine expression or a beautiful idea: if you read poetry to him, he'll exclaim at each delicate expression – 'beautiful!' 'fine!' but can give no reason. Yet he is *always* correct and just in his remarks. He is low in stature – long visage – light hair, coarse features – ungainly – awkward – is a fiddler – loves ale – likes girls – somewhat idle – hates work.

To which the poet Edward Storey adds, 'Allowing for some exaggeration in Drury's description (and he was often guilty of that) there are aspects of Clare's nature which are confirmed both by his own words and those of others. The distinguished features shown in the Behnes Burlowe bust may not have been apparent to Drury who, in those early years, was more accustomed to seeing the twenty-six year old Clare in his labourer's clothes, unkempt, frequently unshaven, clumsy in the presence of strangers, and certainly fond of a few pints as well as girls'.

In 1820, having accepted Clare's poems for publication, John Taylor commissioned William Hilton to paint a portrait of him as part of the launch onto the literary scene. For then as now people liked to know what an author looked like. Hilton and Peter de Wint had been art students together and both were to become Clare's friends. Hilton was to be a doubly unfortunate artist for not only did he not sell but his use of asphaltum, a mixture of coal-tar with sand and chalk, caused his work to decay. Yet his portrait of the young John Clare increasingly haunts our imagination. Here he is as he was when he was first read, and at the beginning of the life we now know so much about. The picture catches the promise, the hesitancy, the Scottish blood, the plight. He wears his best suit and a look of uncertainty. What is plain is the face of a writer. Eight years later John Taylor commissioned a bust of his now celebrated author by Henry Behnes. Henry and William Behnes were sculptor brothers, the sons of a German piano-maker and his English wife. William was said to be the better artist although something of a rake. Henry Behnes, they said, though inferior as a sculptor was less respectable as a person. He redeemed this reputation when cholera swept Rome, where he was studying and paying his way as a bust modeller, by caring for the sick without much thought for himself, and where the disease took him off in 1837. We remember him because he made a bust of Clare.

About this time an anonymous contributor to the Druid's *Monthly Magazine*, in 1833, saw the new poet on the scene and described him thus: 'The first glance of Clare would convince you that he was no common man, he has a head of highly intellectual character, the reflective faculties being exceedingly well-developed; but the most striking feature is the eye, light blue and flashing with the fire of genius ... and his conversation is animated, striking, and full of imagination'.

In April 1829 Clare told his friend Eliza Emmerson, 'I am very glad you like the Bust as I thought myself it was a good one but Frank Simpson [a Stamford friend] tells me he thinks Harry's [Henry Behnes] last touches in my absence did not add any improvements to it but rather injured the freshness of the likeness that he so happily caught in the model and as it was when I first saw it'. The previous year William Behnes was asking Clare to a write a suitable verse for his bust of Princess Victoria. But Clare was ill. 'I wish to accompany your monument yet it is all no use, I can do nothing for the more I try the worse I aim'.

A few years earlier it had all been so different. His learned friend Octavius Gilchrist had guided the famous young poet around London, and shown him the sights. It was springtime. They had lodged above a jeweller's and watchmaker's in the Strand and had walked to Westminster Abbey in the sunshine to see Poets' Corner, not then crowded with novelists. This part of the south transept had begun its literary life when an Oxford undergraduate had found a wrecked grave, that of Geoffrey Chaucer who had died in 1400. It was now 1556. The student collected Chaucer's bones and had them placed in a magnificent tomb with a canopy, the finest now in Poets' Corner, paying for it, they said, himself, and setting in process our honouring of national literary genius. A few feet away on the outside wall Caxton had set up the first English printing press to publish *The Canterbury Tales* and other works. As we have seen, Clare had been loaned Keats's Chaucer. He treasured it. It was the translation (and bowdlerisation) by Cowden Clarke, Keats's headmaster at Enfield. As Clare stood there one of those rushings together of past and present words would have overwhelmed him, something which most writers experience at some time or other.

In the 1980s I became friends with Michael Mayne when he was Vicar of Great St Mary's, Cambridge, a priest who was steeped in English literature and who loved Clare. Michael Mayne became Dean of Westminster shortly after the John Clare Society had been founded.

Silent Likenesses

He knew about Clare's visit to Poets' Corner and one evening when I was staying at the Deanery he said, 'Don't you think that Clare should be there?' The rule was to have a candidate supported by three signatures. I chose those of Ted Hughes, the then Poet Laureate, V. S. Pritchett, President of the Society of Authors, and Angus Wilson, President of the Royal Society of Literature. On the great day Ted Hughes unveiled one of the last stone memorials to be placed in Poets' Corner. Later writers, and some overlooked ones like Herrick and Oscar Wilde, would have their names engraved on windows. John Clare is next to Matthew Arnold for no reason other than space. On it the Abbey Surveyor had carved a bird carrying a sprig of clary, a fanciful interpretation of the poet's name. This plant, *Salvia verbenaca*, wild clary, was once planted on graves during the middle ages in the belief that it conferred immortality on those buried below. Clare would have enjoyed the botanical association but would have not much minded if, as P. H. Reaney's *The Origin of English Surnames* has it, Clare most likely derives from the occupation of clayer, or plasterer. For me it has always had something to do with clarity or Clare in Suffolk, or just bright air filled with language. I had made a huge midsummer cushion out of wild flowers from my fields to lay in Poets' Corner, and the Helpston schoolchildren had brought the descendants of the plants he saw there to his memorial, and we sang his bitter hymn *A Stranger once did bless the earth*, and Ted Hughes read *The Nightingale's Nest*. As Edward Storey said:

> And there you were today,
> your name engraved on stone
> where all the world comes to respect
> a nation's poets – Chaucer,
> Milton, Blake, and those
> who were to follow your brief fame –
> Hopkins, Hardy, and T.S. Eliot.

A decade or more later we are still absorbed in the memorial business as the John Clare Society hands over Tom Bates's plaque of the poet in profile, to be mounted in the new John Clare Lecture Theatre at

At Helpston

Nottingham Trent University. Once John Clare sat for a painter, a sculptor and a photographer who looked deeply into his features. Tom Bates has him in his mind's eye and what he saw now feeds our imagination. In Clare's day there was a passion for likenesses, a longing for more likeness than 'art', for faces could vanish in no time at all. Our knowledge of Keats would have been quite different had not his friend Joseph Severn snatched from oblivion that eager profile.

Shortly after his visit to Poets' Corner Clare wrote to John Taylor, their shared publisher, 'I am very sorry for poor Keats, the symptoms of his illness I think very alarming as we have people in the same way here, often who creep on for a little while – but it generally proves death has struck at the root – for they mostly go off – my only master whom I lived with when a boy at the Blue Bell went off in the same way exactly – be sure to tell Keats to take care of cold and from extreme fatigue this hot weather – I should like to see the fiz of the man before he drops off'.

Phiz was Georgian slang for physiognomy – face, countenance divine. Only the painter, the sculptor, could preserve this look. Clare, old, noble, tidied up, lived into photography. Our contemporary sculptor Anthony Gormley uses his own body, and those of individuals who would in the ordinary way have not been carved or moulded, and who otherwise would have endured only via the camera. Speaking up for sculpture he said that his Angel of the North unconsciously influences everyone who catches a glimpse of it, usually while travelling, although there can be no common analysis of this experience. But sculpture has always been profoundly influential. I once read that Helen Waddell believed her entire future was directed or changed by her having to pass a great Buddha on the way to school. Her parents were Ulster missionaries in China, unaware that their daughter passed daily through an iconic ground of wisdom and serenity. The work of Epstein, Henry Moore, Hepworth, Frink, or some unknown carver of the Christ at Vezeley, or some journeyman maker of a general or politician for the local town square, or some unrecognised by the passer-by true work of art such as the statue of James II outside the National Gallery, or many a war memorial, alters things. Statues can be marvellous, can be preposterous, such as

Silent Likenesses

Saddam's or the communist Dagons which littered eastern Europe, or unworthy of their subject, such as those in many Roman Catholic churches, but they are never negligible. Their power is very strange. Mostly they remain wonderfully interesting. In the lecture theatre, students will catch John Clare's face and look again, will look him up.

The Behnes' bust of John Clare, 1828,
Northampton Central Library

RIDER HAGGARD AND THE DISINTEGRATION OF CLARE'S WORLD

'Nowadays the novel is almost everything. If a matter is to be read of, it must be spiced and tricked out with romance. But, rightly or wrongly, I imagine that the generations to come will study our facts rather than our fiction.' So declared Henry Rider Haggard at the close of the nineteenth century as he exchanged the hat of a bestselling novelist for that of a worried Norfolk farmer. The prognostication would not prove accurate where he was concerned. *King Solomon's Mines*, *She* and a number of his tales bear both reading and examination to this day. Their narrative strength and brilliant imaginative atmosphere, like those of Stevenson and Ballantyne, have kept Haggard's fictions from being carried away on the usual tides. His Africa and his East Anglia were equally potent forces in his literary development, though in severely divided interests. Africa made him an Empire romance-writer of the first water in ordinary popular terms, but two small farms on the Suffolk-Norfolk border made him an agricultural historian not unworthy a place near Arthur Young, William Cobbett and Lord Ernle. Was Haggard himself divided, a part colonialist, part squire? An administrator of the Cape and a JP and churchwarden of his English village, a family man and a wanderer, a progressive abroad and a Tory at home, a man of action in Pretoria and a dreamer in West Bradenham – was his a double life? Curiously not. His personality combining an earthy level-headedness with that uniquely Victorian adventurousness and fantasy was all of a confident piece. Which is why his two 'state of the land' books, *A Farmer's Year* and *Rural England*, are now recognized as key reading for anyone who wants to know how and why the countryside we see today has emerged. Perhaps more novelists should be set to producing reports on social change.

Rider Haggard and the Disintegration of Clare's World

Haggard took as a blueprint for *A Farmer's Year* Thomas Tusser's *Hundredth Good Pointes of Husbandrie*, a practical guide to farming written by a professional musician in the year in which Elizabeth I came to the throne. Tusser wrote his famous advice at Cattawade, Suffolk, where he was sowing and ploughing fields very close to those which would be worked by John Constable's family in the eighteenth century. It is the source of a great number of the rural proverbs, saws and platitudes which are still in use today. Tusser later farmed at West Dereham, Norfolk, which is why he attracted Haggard. Here was a kind of artist whose duty, like his own, it was to understand and explain man's primal toil, the growing and harvesting of crops, and the herding of animals. Except that, unlike Tusser's agricultural scene, Haggard's was one of stagnation, collapse and abandonment. The tragedy was what the politicians and newspapers of his time were calling 'the flight from the land'. When he wrote *Rural England*, he placed a text from the Book of Judges on the title-page—'The highways were unoccupied ... the inhabitants of the villages ceased.'

The epigraph on the title-page of *A Farmer's Year,* the bitter-sweet journal of what was happening on his own farms as the great agricultural depression descended upon them 'during the last year but one of an eventful and wondrous century' comes from Tom Tusser, the musician-farmer struggling along in the 1550s by the River Stour:

> Who minds to quote
> Upon this note
> May easily find enough:
> What charge and pain,
> To little gain
> Doth follow toiling plough.

Haggard called *A Farmer's Year* 'His commonplace book for 1898' and illustrated it with maps, statistical tables and melancholy sepia pictures. He shows that he is a master of 'atmosphere', that here is no less powerful in its way than that which surrounds Ayesha and

155

At Helpston

Umslopogaas. He was in his early forties when he wrote it and was taking stock of his future after having unsuccessfully contested the local parliamentary seat. His career so far had been extraordinary – thrilling even – combining as it did the Victorian virtues of action and the ability to describe it. At nineteen he had sailed to South Africa to be secretary to the Governor of Natal, Sir Henry Bulwer. Two years later he was on the staff of Sir Theophilus Shepstone and had himself raised the Union flag in Pretoria's main square. Revered by the Africans, detested by the Boers, Shepstone had annexed the Transvaal for Britain almost single handed – and without consulting the government. The resulting turmoil ended an extraordinary career. Shepstone's psychological approach to native Africa and his great adventures – he had himself crowned Cetewayo King of Zululand – entranced the young Haggard and fed his imagination. Although he was still only twenty-four when he returned to England for good, Africa and daring radicals like Shepstone continued to influence his vision and made him a very unusual member of Norfolk's farming and sporting gentry. Most curious of all was his ability not to allow his reputation as a popular romancer in any way to compromise that which he was soon to gain as the tough and realistic recorder of Britain's worst agricultural slump. Thus his *Farmer's Year*, a format frequently used by poets, diarists and country-calendarists, is a village book with a difference.

Haggard began farming in 1889, a time when many of those who could were getting out of the industry, and especially the farm-labourers. Throughout East Anglia 'Our American relations were bringing villages to poverty by swamping the markets' – i.e. newly-invented iron grainships, the oil tankers of their day, were flooding Europe with cheap corn from the prairies of the United States and Canada. And if this wasn't bad enough, a run of wet summers which culminated in 'the fearful year of 1879' had washed out what was left of harvests and hope. For Haggard, not long married and also by now fast becoming one of England's most popular writers of adventure fiction, it was not just a question of truthfully documenting the collapse of farming, but of a sincere need to reawaken in country people their belief in nature, in the patterns of field-work and of craftsmanship, and most of all a belief in the superiority of village existence to that of the city. 'What kind places are these cities to live in, for the poor?' What kind of places in the late nineteenth century were Bedingham and Ditchingham for thirteen shillings-a-week farm labourers and near bankrupt farmers? *A Farmer's Year* provides answers that are both earthily practical and filled with Haggard's deep love for the land. A few months before he wrote it he had visited Egypt and had seen the paintings and reliefs on the royal tombs at Sakkara, and had thought how very like he was to 'the gentlemen-farmers of the Fifth and Sixth Dynasties who, whilst yet alive, caused their future sepulchres to be adorned with representations of such scenes of daily life and husbandry as to them were most pleasant and familiar'. Egypt had had plagues, but they passed and the joy of the cornfields remained. So he makes his plea to the English countryman to stand firm, 'although how the crisis will end it is not possible for the wisest among us to guess today'. We now know that this crisis ended in the 1940s, when the nation's food requirements inaugurated the second agricultural revolution – and, subsequently, today's embarrassing food mountains.

In all Haggard farmed 365 acres, some two-thirds of which were near his house at Ditchingham, a big village of 1100 inhabitants, and a third in Bedingham, a village 5 miles distant. Some of the Ditchingham land was rented. These farms are immensely ancient and are mostly on 'loving' or heavy land which clings to boots and wheels. When such farms go down it can take years to drain and weed them and bring them back to good working order, and he records his struggles with the dereliction at Bedingham. Ditchingham, where the young Haggards lived in the Lodge, was a very different matter for the situation was one of the most beautiful in Norfolk, where the Bath Hills and the Waveney Valley spread towards Bungay and the grounds of the Lodge were bordered by the river. Close to the village were the extensive woodlands owned by Lord de Saumarez but whose shooting rights belonged to Haggard. The scene here is that of the successful Empire-builder come home to rest on his laurels – except that it happens to be a scene whose underlying difficulties are preoccupying a landowner novelist whose idealism and expert grasp of agricultural economy

At Helpston

were tearing him apart, emotionally speaking. In time he would produce the kind of report which make governments act, although those of his own day scarcely raised a finger to help the farmer and his men. But now, as the scale of what was happening became clear, Haggard decided that a personal farming diary in the classic form, a book which everybody connected with the land would be warned and inspired by, was essential.

A Farmer's Year holds nothing back. The profit and loss of Ditchingham and Bedingham are given to the last halfpenny. So in another sense are those of Haggard's personality as he swings over from being a typical conservative to a highly candid radical. Much of what he longed to happen has happened, a great deal of what he was sensibly proposing nearly a century ago still hasn't been done. The one thing in particular which the modern reader must be struck by is the gulf which stretches between a Victorian gentleman-farmer and his labourers. As magistrate, employer, church warden and workhouse guardian, Haggard is in total control of them and not less possessive of them than were those Nile farmers of their slaves whose seasonal tasks he saw carved around the doors of Sakkara. He admires their skills and strength, their stoicism and their character, but with all his imagination he cannot get into their situation, and his book is the better, if the more bitter, for his never attempting to do so. Suitably in the December chapter he describes a visit to Heckingham Workhouse and it sums up his absolute honesty.

> What do these old fellows think about, I wonder, as they hobble to and fro round those measureless precincts of bald brick? The sweet-eyed children that they begot and bred up fifty years ago, perhaps, whose pet names they still remember, dead or lost to them for the most part; or the bright waving cornfields whence they scared birds when they were lads from whom death and trouble were yet a long way off. I dare say, too, that deeper problems worry them at times in some dim half-apprehended fashion; at least I thought so when the other day I sat behind two of them in a church near the workhouse. They could not read, and I doubt if they understood much of what was passing, but I observed consideration in their eyes. Of what? Of the terror and the marvel of

existence, perhaps, and of that good God whereof the parson is talking in those long unmeaning words. God ! They know more of the devil and all his works; ill-paid labour, poverty, pain, and the infinite unrecorded tragedies of humble lives. God? They have never found Him. He must live beyond the workhouse wall – out there in the graveyard – in the waterlogged holes which very shortly ...

In all Haggard employs fifteen men on his farm and gives meticulous descriptions of their many skills. Their dogged strength astounds him. In January he watches two of them bush-draining a huge expanse of clay land. It takes ten weeks and at the end 'such toilers betray not the least delight at the termination of their long labour' (*A Farmer's Year*). Similarly with dyke-drawing, the toughest of all the winter jobs. This is a book which reminds one that, the ploughing apart, most of Britain's landscape was fashioned by men with spades. Haggard's men work a twelve-hour day in summer and every daylight hour in winter, and without holidays. Minimal though their education is, it 'teaches them that there are places in the world besides their own Little Pedlington' and makes them aspiring and restless. More and more of them disappear, making for the army, the colonies, the Lowestoft fishing smacks, anywhere preferable to a Norfolk farm. It grieves him. *A Farmer's Year* is his apology for agriculture as man's natural activity, the noblest of tasks, and he cites its improved conditions. Now and then, as in Africa, he joins in the labour, although this he finds separates him further from the workers than if he merely sat on his horse and made notes. What ever he sees or feels or does is written down with total candour, and his journal is at once an important and authoritative compendium of farming practice, a private confessional, a history of turn of the century Norfolk and, in its way, an entertainment. The scene he paints is darker than he wants it to be and, for something which set out as an autobiographical rural calendar about the state of the land at a given date, balance sheets and all, there are highly emotional and intellectual tensions of an unexpected kind.

Sir Henry Rider Haggard's then radical exposure of agrarian decline in this and other books disturbed the profoundly conservative rural

At Helpston

society to which he belonged, and, getting on for a hundred years later, it is still capable of upsetting us. But capable of delighting us too, for this is a rich picture of the old landscape and the 'old' people as they were before modern farming and other developments transformed both. It is unlikely to make anyone nostalgic but it will, like a tale by Thomas Hardy, remind us of the tensions, and of the idyll, which not so very long ago were interlocked, as it were, in the fields.

A Farmer's Year first appeared as a serial before it was published in book form in 1899. Its purpose was to hearten the yeomen of England during a time of utter hopelessness and to check the abandonment of the villages by their employees. Haggard pours into the narrative everything which would fascinate the farmer and his men: legends, local history, flowers, sport, the church, games, gossip, weather, prices, customs, country pleasures, hard-nosed profits and losses – nothing is left out. He said that 'it mirrors faithfully ... the decrepit and even dangerous state of farming and attendant industries in eastern England during the great agricultural crisis of the last decade of the nineteenth century', and it does.

Raindrops after frost

The only known photograph of John Clare, taken by
W.W. Law in 1862, two years before the poet's death

Three Jays

SELECT BIBLIOGRAPHY

Bate, Jonathan, *John Clare: A Biography*, Picador, 2003
Blythe, Ronald, *Talking About John Clare*, Trent Books, 1999
Blythe, Ronald, *A Writer's Day-Book*, Trent Editions, 2006
Beckett, R.B., *John Constable's Correspondence*, Boydell, 1976
Blunden, Edmund (Ed), *Sketches in the Life of John Clare by Himself*, Cobden-Sanderson, 1931
Goodridge, John (Ed), *The Independent Spirit: John Clare and the Self-Taught Tradition*, John Clare Society, 1994
Grainger, Margaret (Ed), *The Natural History Prose Writings of John Clare*, Oxford University Press, 1983
John Clare Society Journal
John Clare Society Newsletter
Robinson, Eric & Summerfield, Geoffrey (Eds), *John Clare, The Shepherd's Calendar*, Oxford University Press, 1964
Robinson, Eric & Powell, David (Eds), *The Poems of John Clare*, Oxford University Press, 1964-84
Sinclair, Iain, *Edge of the Orison*, Hamish Hamilton, 2005
Storey, Edward, *A Right to Song: The Life of John Clare*, Methuen, 1982
Taylor, Basil, *Constable: Paintings, Drawings and Watercolours*, Phaidon, 1973
Thornton, Kelsey, *John Clare: The Rural Muse*, Carcanet, 1982
Tibble, J.W. & Anne (Eds), *The Letters of John Clare*, Routledge & Kegan Paul, 1951

Two starlings fighting

INDEX OF PEOPLE AND PLACES

Acton, Suffolk 68
Aldeburgh 66
Allen, Matthew 31, 91
Arnold, Matthew 86, 151
Artis, Edmund 63, 71
Austen, Jane 71

Balboa, Vasco de Nunez 17
Baring-Gould, Sabine 52
Barker, Thomas 40
Barrett, Hugh 29
Barrett, Roderic 32
Bate, Jonathan 72, 84
Bates, Tom 151-2
Becker, Harry 57
Bedingham 157-8
Behns, Henry 149-50
Behns, William 149
Bell, Adrian 79, 35, 121
Bennett, Sterndale 30
Benton End 13,15
Beresford-Jones, Mary 107
Bewick, Thomas 75, 115
Billings Brothers 59
Black Mountain 29
Blake, William 89
Bloomfield, Robert 35-38, 41-2, 47, 58, 77, 89, 133
Blunden, Edmund 35, 49, 58-60, 99
Blythe, George 16
Blythe, Matilda 16
Borrow, George 85
Boswell, Gordon 82
Boswell, James 102
Bottengoms Farm 15, 28, 32, 39, 47, 61, 70

Bridges, Robert 138
Bristol 39
Britten, Benjamin 30
Brooke, Rupert 65
Brown, William 101
Browne, Sir Thomas 89
Bulwer, Sir Henry 156
Bunyan, John 94, 120-2
Burke, Edmund 36
Burlowe, Behns 149
Burns, Robert 28, 31-2, 88, 90, 101, 103, 110

Calvino, Italo 66
Calypso's Isle 15, 18
Cambridge 13
Carr, J L 137
Casterton 33, 74
Cattawade 155
Causley, Charles 52, 60
Chapman, George 14-17, 61
Charsfield 80
Chaucer, Geoffrey 76, 150
Chilcott, Timothy 56-7
Clare, Suffolk 67
Clare, Alice 102, 107
Clare, Martha (Patty) 90-1
Clare, Parker 33, 45
Clarke, Cowden 87, 150
Cobbett, William 154
Colchester 59-60, 65
Coleridge, S 40, 139, 145
Collins, William 76
Constable, Abram 43, 46
Constable, Golding 41, 45
Constable, John 37-39, 42, 44-5

165

At Helpston

Copley, Ian 30
Corri, Haydn 29
Cowper, William 77
Crabbe, George 17, 127
Crossan, Greg 139
Cudmore, Alan 13, 19
Curtis, William 75

Darwin, Charles 60-1
Deakin, Roger 45
De Wint, Peter 149
Discoed 28
Ditchingham 157-8
Dodgson, Stephen 30
Douglas, Keith 49
Druce, Dr 66
Drury, Edward 148-9

East Anglia 36, 154-6
East Bergholt 38, 44
Elton, Sir Charles 39-40
Elton, Lady 39
Emerson, Eliza 56, 58, 74, 150
Enfield 15, 87
Epping 32, 40, 86, 126, 142
Ernle, Lord 43, 154
Essex 42, 87

Fens 32, 42
Fisher, John 44
Fitzgerald, Edward 60, 84
Flatford Mill 43
Forster E M 92

Gainsborough, Thomas 148
Gallipoli 35
Garrett, Denis 13
Garrett, Jane 13
Gaudia-Brezska 57
Gay, John 76
Gilchrist, Octavius 153
Gittings, Robert 88

Glinton 72, 123, 142
Goodridge, John 103
Gormley, Anthony 152
Grafton, Duke of 36
Grainger, Margaret 24, 59, 60, 75, 93, 125, 133, 143, 145
Gray, John 76
Gray, Thomas 77
Gregory, Francis 131-3
Greig, John 38
Grigson, Geoffrey 99, 138
Groom, Robert Hindes 84

Haggard, Sir Henry Rider 99, 154, 160
Hallam, Arthur 40
Hardy, Thomas 33, 35, 62, 71, 88-100, 125, 127, 143
Hayes, William 75
Hazlitt, William 20, 59, 73, 74, 115
Heaney, Seamus 47, 131, 143
Heckingham Workhouse 158
Henderson, Joseph 25, 71, 75
Herbert, George 29
Herrick, Robert 151
High Beach 19, 86, 105
Hilton, William 149
Hölderlin, Friedrich 65
Holst, Gustav 118
Hold, Trevor 28-9
Homer 14-17
Honington 35
Hopkins, Gerard Manley 138, 142, 145
Hughes, Ted 47, 142-3, 151

Jagger, Mick 49
Jenner, Edward 38
Job 26
Johnson, Samuel 102
Joyce, Mary 23, 34, 107, 112, 126

166

Index

Kapp, Xavier 67
Keats, John 14-15, 17-18, 61, 76, 87, 89, 142, 150, 152
Keyes, Sidney 49, 57, 74
Kent, Elizabeth 75
Kilvert, Francis 19, 29
King's Lynn 39

Lamb, Charles 40
Langland, William 118
Lear, Edward 39
Lemprier, John 16
Lewis, Alun 49
Loftt, Capel 36, 133
Lolham Briggs 22
London 14, 39
Long Melford 13, 59, 65, 69
Lugg, River 28

Mabey, Richard 47
Macfarlane, Robert 14
Mann, Mary 95
Mallarmé, Stephen 66
Mayne, Michael 150
Millay, Edna St Vincent 66
Milton, Lord 71, 75

Nash, John 13
Nayland 14
Newmarket 70
New Forest 45
Norfolk 154, 159
Northamptonshire 32, 61
Northampton Lunatic Asylum 30-32, 91, 99, 109
Northborough 22

Ocean, East Anglia's Romany 80
Offa's Dyke 29

Parker, John 102, 107
Passchendael 67

Perkens, Mrs 13
Peterborough 66, 67, 70
Pickworth 84, 122
Poetry of the Year 1867 68, 132
Porter, Alan 66
Presteigne 29
Pritchett, V S 151
Puxon, Grattan 82

Radstock, Lord 56, 74, 77
Ramsay, John 106
Rannoch Moor 101
Reaney, P H 151
Rilke, Rainer Maria 65
Rippingille, Edward 39-40
Robinson, Eric 30-31, 99
Royce Wood 22
Rubbra, Edmund 30
Ryhall 122

Sakkara 157-8
Sassoon, Siegfried 13, 59, 65, 67
Scotland 32
Scott, John 40
Scott, Sir Walter 103, 108
Selborne 21
Shaw, Martin 30
Shakespeare, William 16, 29, 76
Sinclair, Iain 13
Sketches in the Life of John Clare by Himself 68
Skrimshire, Dr Fenwick 72
Smart, Christopher 76
Smith, Anthony 49
South Africa 154, 156
Southey, Robert 40
Stamford 25
Stansfield 68
Stockenny Farm 28-9
Storer, James 38
Storey, Edward 13, 28, 29, 60
Sudbury 148

At Helpston

Summerfield, Geoffrey   99
Swing, Captain   44
Symons, Arthur   66

Tannahill, Robert   105-6
Taplin, Kim   117
Taylor and Hessey   21, 24, 28, 40, 55, 56, 57, 76
Tennyson, Alfred   40, 91, 132

Thomas, R H   51
Thomson, James   36, 42, 73, 132
Thornton, Kelsey   103
Tibble, J W   40, 99
Traherne, Thomas   29
Turner, James   52
Turnill, John   133
Tusser, Thomas   156

Vaughan, Henry   29
Verlaine, Paul   66
Vestris, Madame   29

Waddell, Helen   152
Waltham Abbey   40
Warlock, Peter   30
Waveney Valley   157
West Bradenham   155
Westminster Abbey   30, 150
White, Gilbert   24-5, 55, 75
White Kirke, Henry   61
Williams, Vaughan   85
Wilson, Sir Angus   151
Wisbech   39
Woodforde, James   114
Wordsworth, Dorothy   40, 118
Wordsworth, William   40, 61, 73, 77, 118, 139
Wormingford   37

Young, Andrew   117, 154

right red
air force blue
oronet of blue & black dots
wings waxy sky blue
paynes grey
black
sharp apricot
wings trans seeming dark
less black furry
smaller variety
blue green delicata
emerald
small reflecting the sky
orange edge
glowing green